A Woman's Voice

A Woman's Voice

A Handbook to Successful
Private and Public Speaking

DOROTHY URIS

STEIN AND DAY/*Publishers*/New York

For Mimi

and

all my sisters

Acknowledgments

Special credit is due to:

Sophia Delza, dancer, teacher, artist, who created the drawings in Chapters 2 and 3

Frances Moore Lappé, whose book *Diet for a Small Planet* has sold half a million copies and helped inspire the speech on food in Chapters 12 and 13

Marya Mannes, author, critic, and speaker, who contributed her original speech "Can a Woman Be President?" to Chapter 13

Alberto Vecchio, teacher of body movement, whose techniques form the basis of exercises for release of nervous tension in Chapters 2 and 3

Grateful acknowledgment is made for permission to reprint works or excerpts of works by the following authors:

Aristophanes, *Lysistrata.*
Translated in an acting version by Gilbert Seldes.
Farrar & Rhinehart, 1930.

Lillian Hellman, *Pentimento.*
Copyright © 1973 by Lillian Hellman.
From *Pentimento* by Lillian Hellman.
By permission of Little, Brown & Co.

Erica Jong, "Alcestis on the Poetry Circuit."
From *Half Lives* by Erica Jong.
Copyright © 1971, 1972, 1973 by Erica Mann Jong.
Reprinted by permission of Holt, Rinehart & Winston, Inc.

Eve Merriam, "Rummage" and "A Charm for Our Time."
Copyright © 1973 by Eve Merriam.
From *Out Loud*.
Used by permission of Atheneum Publishers.

Dorothy Parker, "L'Envoi."
Copyright 1926, renewed 1954 by Dorothy Parker.
Reprinted by permission of the Viking Press, Inc.

George Bernard Shaw, *Saint Joan*.
Reprinted by permission of The Society of Authors, on behalf of
the Bernard Shaw Estate.

Gertrude Stein, "Storyette H.M."
From *Portraits and Prayers* by Gertrude Stein.
Copyright 1934 and renewed 1962 by Alice B. Toklas.
Reprinted by permission of Random House, Inc.

May Swenson, "All That Time."
From *Half Sun Half Sleep* by May Swenson.
Copyright © 1967 by May Swenson.
Used by permission of the author.

Louis Untermeyer, *A Treasury of Laughter*.
Copyright © 1946 by Louis Untermeyer.
Reprinted by permission of Simon & Schuster.

Marta Vivas, "Feminism in New York."
From *The New York Woman's Directory*.
Copyright © 1973 by Womanpower Project.
Reprinted by permission of Workman Publishing Co., New York
City.

Contents

guage. Speech melodies and what they tell. Take a poetry break. Purposeful negative practice.

1

About a Woman's Voice

Two questions: Why another book on speaking? and Why for women? Let's tackle them one at a time.

To begin with, must we still cite the reasons for speaking better? Effective speaking has been tied to personal success from way back, before the first speech book came off a hand press. And not nearly that long ago Dale Carnegie's *How to Win Friends and Influence People* (by speaking better) sold millions of copies. Now we have a best seller selling the idea that we're our *own* best friends and, presumably, do a lot of talking to ourselves. And this is a time in which *dialogue with others* is ever more urgent.

The latest speech textbooks, in glossy softcover, are a grab bag of academic subjects and trendy communication titles—frequently in warmed-over editions. How removed such books are from the lives and concerns of the very people who voice them!

Techniques in the abstract skirt the real problems of speech competence. The study of voice and diction has become an only-for-actors subject; the rest of us evidently have to make do with the cozy snare of "just be natural." So-called normal speech remains the area of neglect.

In short, we need books *beamed to individual needs and creativity,* and with content responsive to this time and place and condition of our communicating lives.

Why a speech book for women? The answers to the first question have half answered this one, if we accept the premise that a book on speaking should relate specifically to the speakers—to the personal

13

problems that women encounter in their life and work styles. The general principles of spoken communication discussed throughout these pages apply, of course, to men as well as women, young as well as old, black as well as white. Speech, after all, is a heterosexual subject.

However, men's longtime experience as active contenders in business and professional arenas has armed their speech with the techniques and the confidence that many women as yet lack. Does this imply that men per se speak well? Obviously not, but since they have for years grown more inured to the public scene, their tones do not carry the psychological load that women's do.

Mingled with women's urge to join freely in today's upswing lurk our built-in habit patterns, programmed by early conditioning, then reinforced by repetition and a reluctance to break with the past. Although there are many attractive female voices and able speakers everywhere (no section of the country has a monopoly on good or bad speech), much too often voice and words lag behind aspirations and accomplishments. Emotional hang-ups from the past exert a strong backward pull.

Here are some exposed voice types revealing psychological restraints that have to be overcome:

—"*When I was a child, I spake as a child* . . . when I became a man [woman], I put away childish things." This voice was not put away as the Bible advises, and as the girl-child grew, the voice did not. Persisting into middle age, high childish accents come close to caricature. Is this rushed, immature speech a shield for "don't expect too much of me"?

—*The housebound voice*, exhausted from lack of adult conversation; listless, with a breathy trailing tune, uncertain of where to settle. (Passively she intones, "Yes, dear . . . no, dear . . . don't forget your rubbers, dear.")

—*Inaudible at ten paces*, accompanied by nervous little gulps of air, supersoft "ladylike" intonation, harking back to her children-should-be-seen-and-not-heard upbringing; the all too common thin voice line; unless corrected, this weak, unsupported instrument is forever inadequate to the demands made upon it.

—*One-way current*, the flat nasal sound in a monotonous rhythm of endless talk; an escape valve for anxiety. On and on goes the voice that seems prematurely aged. A habitual constriction (back-of-the-throat uptightness) produces this nasalized whine. Only strong resolve will cut off such appetite for monologue.

—*Overcompensating tones,* born of frustration, short on self-esteem, given to shrill verbal aggression, beating up herself and her voice. Such aggressive energy cries for a positive outlet.

—*The sultry, smoky voice,* synonymous with sex, calculated to quicken the male pulse; she's a victim of illusion, and probably of damaged vocal cords from pressuring her tones downwards. (Surely, sexiness is in the ear of the listener/beholder. How else explain the legendary allure of the little-girl voice, a Marilyn Monroe derivative, and the husky sophisticate sound, a Greta Garbo holdover?)

—*The "going public" syndrome,* personified by the campaigning zeal of involved women from Maine to California, shifting suddenly from private to public speaking. Their bottled-up, high-keyed enthusiasm turns coarse or strident. Despite splendid goals, such voices turn people off.

Do these profiles shed light on some of the problems plaguing our daily talk? HELP WANTED: a planned program, *supportive* of the special character of woman's communication at all levels of experience, to *enhance their private speaking* and *public skills.*

Double Standard Talk

Women have also to contend with prejudicial attitudes toward their speech, like this negative reflex: if you talk like a woman, you sound like a magpie; if you lower your pitch, you're imitating a man!

A kind of folklore of female language still prevails in jokes, cartoons, and TV programs—to wit: we talk too much, endlessly in fact. And the content? You guessed it: silly, emotional, vague. Female inflections tend to turn answers into questions, as if to avoid commitment.

There's some basis to all this; nevertheless, speech "tunes" that convey uncertainty can and do change when women detect and correct an upglided inflection in their answers. Example: "What's your name?" Answer: "Mary Smith . . . ?" The listener's reaction: Isn't she sure? Obviously, Mary should change her tune and level that ascending curve. (When more self-assertive, she will.)

Sonorous and masculine, the media's "voice of authority" is the voice that sells and, apparently, excels. The persuasive *voice-over* behind the TV commercials is still predominantly male. Poised and sharpened, women's talk techniques on TV are just as telling as men's—not the same, but equal.

No identity crisis. Improving speech habits or any other inadequacy should not imply, as some fear, a rejection of the past. The reality is that earlier speech behavior doesn't work in adult life: we cannot make a firm statement in weak, uncertain tones. In the physical effort of consciously strengthening our voices, we reach for the emotional certainty that our message must carry. And as rigid patterns begin to unwind along with psychological snags, we are freed to realize a greater potential. Speech *liberates.*

Other hang-ups—the challenge of change, the worry of sounding "different," the fancied ridicule of peer groups, the intimidation of an articulate husband—these and other qualms will lessen in the *doing,* in the process of building a freer and stronger speech personality.

"Necessity's Sharp Pinch . . ."

With women's ever-rising status, good speaking has become a bread-and-butter matter. Necessity dictates change and demands that women of many diverse backgrounds shape up their speech skills with words that match deeds and voices that make good listening. Women have plenty of motivation to do so, especially in a time of stepped-up competition.

Today's woman has been breaking and covering ground at such a clip that it would seem that yesterday's statistics need constant revision to meet tomorrow's deadline. In the widening range of roles she plays, each is a *speaking* part; few walk-ons are available.

Many of our youngest women feel free to move in many directions, geographically and professionally; with the overriding theme self-fulfillment, they have high expectations and mean to *use* their education (merely being employed is not enough).

Their speech? The girlish voices need body, not mike amplification; the rapid talk supports too much "in" slang—redundant, like dirty denims. They should abandon the dead end of political cynicism, *speak out and be heard* with language that communicates beyond age barriers.

Women in the suburban dreamhome are out rather than in. They can be found in the vanguard of volunteer workers as advocates for conservation, pollution control, and consumer rights, as political activists, and avid students. The *volunteer professional* is no longer a contradiction in terms. Many women have crossed over into paid jobs; others have run successfully for local offices. Despite the slick ads, housewives are not spending all their time soaking in the bathtubs of the nation.

Their speech? It varies considerably and is often less than good. Unquestionably, their upward mobility would improve along with *improved communication* in and out of the home.

Regardless of the commercial, "You're not getting older, you're getting better," women with grown children on their own often feel like nonpersons; their energies clamor for recycling. And with today's mandatory early retirement, only a minority of older women is permitted to be productive in professions and jobs.

All the latest medical advances (from hormone replacement to vitamins) contribute to a heightened vigor at ever increasing age levels. The same holds true for *voice age.* The prescription: specific speech exercises to energize the vocal instrument regularly, keeping it fit and flexible. A mature talent to reach out to people with conversational ease is an invaluable asset.

An Assist from History

Today's active women are not brand-new. They've been building upon a two-hundred-year history of role models who, in vastly more difficult times, spoke their enlightened minds against injustice and discrimination and for their own rights as citizens.

Some eloquent voices from the past:

Abigail Adams, wife of John Adams, second president of the United States: "He [Mr. Adams] is very saucy to me in return for a list of female grievances which I transmitted to him. . . . I even threatened fomenting a Rebellion in case we were not considered, and assured him we would not hold ourselves bound by any laws in which we had neither a voice nor representation." (1776)

Elizabeth Cady Stanton, answering newspapers' objections to women's conventions: "There is no such thing as a sphere for a sex. When Angelina Grimké and Lucretia Mott [hold forth in public] with eloquence and power on slavery and women's rights, who shall tell us that these divinely inspired women are out of their sphere?" (1848)

Elizabeth Blackwell, first woman in the United States to be granted a medical degree: "My whole life is devoted unreservedly to the service of my sex. The study and practice of medicine is in my thought but one means to [that] great end . . ." (1848)

Sojourner Truth, crusading ex-slave: "Ain't I a woman? Look at me . . . I could work as much and eat as much as a man—when I could get it—and bear the lash as well. I have borne thirteen children and seen most sold off to slavery. When I cried out with my mother's grief, none but Jesus heard me. But ain't I a woman?" (1853)

Mrs. Ben Hooper, lobbying for women's suffrage in Wisconsin: "I traveled over a good deal of distance talking the question out with politically prominent men. . . . Some days I got up at 5:30 . . . and did not get home until midnight. . . . In Appleton it was 10 below, in Marinette . . . I had to wade through snow up to the tops of my shoes." (1915)

Over the years, women have developed special talents and qualities. Thanks to the current momentum, all of these promise to reach full bloom: a faculty for *organizing people,* an innate gift for *interpersonal relationships,* an ability to get to the *nub of questions,* and a *no-nonsense approach* to problem solving. Underlying all is the greater value that women, in their compassion for humanity, attach to human life.

The 1960s' crusade by a handful of feminists tapped a deep source of emerging change, what came to be called the Women's Movement. The lib° controversy has been simmering down. Most women stayed out of the argument and, responding to the historic impulse, many just went ahead to new or revitalized jobs or professions and expanded life-styles. Every day a tradition topples; this fact is taken

---

° The term *lib,* short for *liberation,* has made it to the dictionary—Webster's New World Dictionary, Second College Edition, © 1972.

for granted, with few bows to the "movers and shakers," and female striving goes forward on other fronts.

Everybody talks—so what? Of all our natural endowments, the speech mechanism is probably the one most taken for granted. We undervalue and misunderstand the message of good speech. Take that old dodge still with us, "I don't want to sound affected." Far from implying c*lahss*-conscious pronunciation, good speech in today's context means *speaking plainly,* with *pleasing voice, attractive rhythm,* and *expressive, useful words.*

Just mention some tonal blemish and defensive attitudes immediately come to the fore. From the voice with a crunch on the vocal cords, "Oh, it's that chest cough." From the voice with a twang, "It's my allergy." From the breathy syllable-swallower, "I'm just awfully tired today," and the most common cop-out of all, "Well, it's the voice I was born with."

Excuses, remember, are designed to impress yourself first of all; they keep you tied to habit and illusion, standing between you and self-realization. When enough discontent with the status*less* quo sets in, the way opens for change and personal growth.

Self-confidence is not enough. The new self-assurance many women have gained is all to the good. Others, feeling the lack, go on wishing, "If I only had more self-confidence . . . ," as if that were all.

How comforting if all one had to do were to tread the path to the analyst's couch or the less expensive chair of group therapy. We could then "just talk out" our talking problems. For, although psyches may improve, speech traits usually remain rooted in the personality. Why? Because speaking is primarily a *muscular* activity. The *body's* mechanism has to learn new physical coordinations and unlearn old ones. How liberating finally to realize that the basis of speech is physical.

Lack of awareness is the number one speech problem.

With the awakening of *speech consciousness,* the moment arrives to investigate the means to deal with incompetent voices: inaudible, tensed-up, or monotonous; and slipshod speaking: slurred, hesitant, or inarticulate. For each of these hindrances there *is* a corrective.

Self-confidence comes straight from know-how, from acquired speech skills that bring abundant rewards throughout the entire range of communicating activity from conversation to solo speaking. Women can infuse such skills with person-to-person content—a distinct advantage.

Just as an artist begins a portrait by sketching in the outlines, so childhood chatter forms the basis of speech personality. With growth and maturity come detail and depth, until characteristic features emerge to identify *you*, the individual.

Your speaking reflects your total life experience, but, unlike the artist's portrait, yours can continue to change. The removal of old shortcomings and the addition of new expertise will fortify from without and bring security within.

Nevertheless, your self-portrait remains unfinished; *life* is the laboratory for continuous exploration. "I had speech in college," some people insist, as if that were that. You never just *have* speech; you *go on* having it.

A Here-and-Now Program

Granted an awareness of why and how, are you ready for the *doing?* Only those who are ready, willing, and able to apply themselves seriously to this book's program will capture fresh insights and triumphant results, whether by acquiring new aptitudes or by polishing old ones.

We present a positive working plan for women, which covers a wide span of speech situations and activities. Our all-pervading aim is to promote proficiency and ease of expression—a day-to-day challenge. Sensitive to women's special needs, the approach is devoted to surmounting the weaknesses and sustaining the strengths of women as communicators.

The chapters follow a charted progression from voice and speech aids (basic sounds, pronunciation, vocabulary) to sophisticated how-to's (interviews, lectures, TV talks, campaigning), thus heightening the ability to reason and discuss.

As you first leaf through the pages, the material most significant for you will catch your eye. Individual interests can be isolated and studied, since the separate sections stand alone.

Do you expect to attend a meeting? Then zero in on "Roberta's Rules of Order." Or perhaps a conference is in the offing? Check with "Dynamics of Discussion." Do you feel tense after a rough day? Try some vocal refreshment by reading aloud from a selection of enlivening material, either poetry or prose. Once familiar with the format, you can choose a self-oriented program.

Our handbook provides practice routines, both functional and lively, though not once-over-lightly success formulas. We start with what turns out to be most difficult for most people: the nitty-gritty of speech improvement, those essential exercises for producing clear voice tones. To begin with, don't be strung out by rules; just bear in mind that if you mean to overcome a given weakness, you have to take on the basic how-to's to reach the important what-for's.

Should you want to investigate how to prepare for an interview or perhaps for a TV talk, go right to the specific material for the help you seek. Don't feel you must first tackle your less than perfect voice, pronunciation, or vocabulary. The exercises will keep.

A Woman's Voice was conceived for women—for *you*—because women have to surmount hurdles that arise simply from their status as women. Each woman is an unrepeatable experiment, one of a kind, an original. Each seeks self-renewal the better to express herself and shape her world.

Many American women, headed where the action is, found their voices on the way. Others already had theirs and have spoken in public, and in private, for years with articulate and dynamic style. Such accomplished, clear-voiced speakers would gladly acknowledge that even a Stradivarius needs tunimg.

Then there are these: If Ms. X hits the jackpot in the fashion world as designer of a brand-new look, if Ms. Y marries the world king of shipping, if Ms. Z becomes a foremost mathematical physicist— should they worry how they sound?

For the great majority of us, however, an unappealing speech personality means running a lifelong obstacle race, one leg hobbled and one arm tied. Women have conquered obstacles beyond expectation in fields that were exclusive male bastions: sports, industry, science, engineering, and on and on. Are speech habits to be the last stronghold of resistance?

Well, we've come a long way, baby. Life has reconstructed societal patterns, and old molds have to go. (*Physical* measures will help pry them loose.) The pull of the present will overcome the drag of the past; the present is, in fact, your best friend.

So, whoever you are, *begin,* and though the going may not always be entertaining, there is nothing more rewarding than speaking your own language with clarity and strength. Raw recruit or seasoned veteran, every area of your life will respond to the stimulus.

PART ONE

Freeing Your Voice

2

Starting Out

An actress's character kit for the parts she plays holds a collection of voice types that, apparently, imitate our weaknesses and strengths (art imitating nature). To bring reality to a given role, the actress works hard to make the tonal quality fit the character like her skin.

To play a complaining character, she simulates a nasal whine; add a shortness of breath, and you have a chronic invalid. Rich resonance reveals the voice of authority; tremulous hesitance, the voice of insecurity. A rasp bespeaks nervous exasperation, while a modulated quality soothes with patience. A monotonous pitch is tied to the colorless individual; flexible tones to the imaginative one.

Are voice characteristics true to life? Are women really like their voices? Probably not, though the vocal signature can surely give the right or wrong impression. Not everyone hangs around long enough to discover the heart of gold beneath a distracting fault.

We have much to learn from the expert actress/communicator: conversational skills displayed in her dialogues, rapport over the telephone (even with no one at the other end), ability to engage her listeners with person-to-person concentration, and her pleasing and unaffected American speech.

The question, But who wants to be an actress? is off the point. Rather ask, Is verbal facility strictly for pros? Is a healthy body solely for tennis champions? Or are good looks just for an actress?

Reject such notions and discover the answer in revitalizing your own self-expression—not with dexterous, professional voice changes but with lasting improvement, achieved offstage. *These setting-up drills for the voice are fashioned for Everywoman.*

Releasing Tension

Forever hammered at us, the word *relax* appears to have lost all meaning. Big-city Americans surely sound more tense than their counterparts in the rest of the world. The full-throated voices of European women may well stir female envy in this country.

Give us credit, though. We do work hard at relaxation. Unhappily we seem only to succeed in accumulating added jitters, seeking relief in tranquilizers, psychotherapy, spectator sports, and other, less beneficial, outlets.

However, certain degrees of muscular tension maintain us upright. If we let go completely, we'd fall on our faces. Relaxation can be correctly defined as that desirable state in which muscle has only as much tension as required for freedom of action. What we need to banish is *tenseness,* the condition that interferes with circulation, knots muscles, and causes discomfort and pain.

As women talk, for every tensely drawn breath, they tend to emit tensely produced sounds, with unpleasant pitches and uneasy rhythms. What concerns us specifically is excessive tension in neck, head, and shoulders, those zones closely related to voice production. By reducing outer strain, we permit inner muscles of the voice box the freedom to function. Besides, a feeling of ease in the speech musculature spreads like balm through your whole body.

Exercises designed to release pressured areas of neck and head should follow a necessary progression for best results:

Set the stage for these and other exercises with a mirror and a permanent chair the right height for you. Most chairs are too high for women. Buy one or cut one down so your legs are at right angles to the floor with feet flat.

How you look and feel. Sit tall, legs comfortably apart and parallel; hands folded, palms up; face in repose (no furrows in forehead); eyes straight ahead facing into the mirror; shoulders down. This is a *naturally* released and becoming posture.

Practice these easeful movements in sequence, as directed. To start right off with a deep head roll may invite pain. Work up to it. All the exercises begin and end at centers, so imagine a straight line down the center of your body.

1. *The nods.* The magic number is eight. Picture a pie, cut into eight sections. Head at front center (first slice), nod; move to the second slice, nod. After the fifth (at back center) continue around the other side until the eighth slice, again at front center. Reverse the sequence. This routine lends you a queenly air, as if you are nodding to acknowledge applause.

2. *Head rests.* Sitting in a chair, shoulders down, incline your head to one side, as if resting it on an air pillow, and just lie there for eight counts. Return to center (always). Now repeat on the other side. Then let your head fall forward; next ease it straight back, but *not too far.* Change directions and continue, all with the same count. (See Fig. 1.)

Figure 1

3. *The small circle.* Rotate your head smoothly all the way around and back to center (eight counts). If you watch for the whites of your eyes in the mirror, your head won't drop too low. Alternate and continue within the small radius until most of the kinks have gone.

4. *The large circle.* With eyes closed, rotate the head more deeply. (Counting "one thousand, two thousand," etc., to "eight thousand," will slow you.) If you feel a painful spot, pause and pass it again back and forth soothingly until it ebbs. Then complete the circle. As your head reaches backward, take care not to constrict the vocal cords. Test the voice. If it sounds constrained, you've gone too far. Change directions and go again.

Now move within a still larger circle. This time bring the shoulders into play as well until the whole upper torso joins in. Alternate: first right, then left. Keep circling in slow rhythm as if even the force of gravity were letting go. With this "in-orbit" sensation, empty your mind and stop forming or even thinking of words.

5. *Sigh to your heart's content.* Lie on the rug, flat on your stom-

ach, your body stretched out with one arm on the floor above your head, the other at your side. Elbows are soft, knees relaxed. Turn your head toward the lowered arm, cheek resting on the floor. Place a small pillow under your head and another under your body between navel and pelvis. Sink yourself into the floor. Be conscious of letting go.

Begin a series of soundless sighs, as if exhausted. Inhaling and exhaling on the sigh, you can feel the abdominal muscles expanding and contracting on the pillow against the floor's hard surface. By degrees, make your sighs *audible* with natural, unforced sound. Change sides and repeat. (See Fig. 2.)

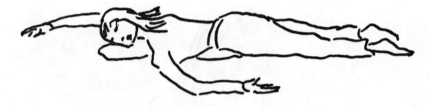

Figure 2

These nods, circles, rolls, and sighs form a useful basic drill to alleviate daily stresses. Before, during, or after the working day, find practice time for the comfort these drills provide, whenever and wherever possible.

What your body learns: Overall ease, the relief of deep sighs, unpressured vibration of sound, and correct breathing for speech.

The Good Breath

The concept of breathing has become something of a mystique in rituals often borrowed from some Eastern religion. The spiritual overtones of such exercises may well bring comfort to hyped American nerves. Our procedure is entirely physical, however. It is designed to build inherent strength for speaking and is comparable to developing that good right (or left) arm essential for tennis or bowling.

Obviously, without intake of air there would be no speech, or anything else for that matter. In fact, we need precious little air to speak with; most people use too much, and not, as they often imagine, too little. The breath gets the vocal machinery going, and an efficient puff of the stuff will do the job. The body's hookup takes over to produce the sounds we utter.

Should you take a deep breath? We all know how—or do we? Gather strength, fill up from abdomen to shoulders, and tighten all the way: we're 100 per cent wrong. For the "Good Breath," the air is indeed drawn in *deeply* yet *economically*. Once mastered, this correct breathing is hardly visible on the surface of the body, since the natural apparatus works on the inside.

Shallow respiration, or "brassiere breathing" (since women are more prone to do this than men), comes with a chest rise and fall, extra helpings of oxygen, and, frequently, active shoulders as well. This style of breathing probably harks back to the cinched-in waist and high corset line of the past. In this period of liberated waistlines (and bustlines), it's time to develop truly functional breathing.

The Progression to the Good Breath

1. Begin by yawning, that classic release for speaking and singing. Press lips gently together, drop the jaw at the same time, then close your eyes, and you'll probably start one coming.

2. As you yawn (or pretend to), stretching the back of your throat with mouth open, can you feel muscles pulling simultaneously deep in your body?

3. Keeping jaw released, begin breathing in and out through the mouth with an even rhythm like a pendulum. (See Fig. 3.)

4. Use a voiceless sound, *ah-ha* (in/out), the sound of breathing without tone. With *ah-ha* in your ears, you can monitor the regular count of this exercise.

5. To help implant the even breathing rhythm, move an arm back and forth with wrists and elbows fluid, as if conducting.

6. After *ah-ha*-ing for a while, can you recapture, by inhaling and exhaling, the same sensation you felt in the lower abdomen when you were yawning? If not, yawn again, and repeat the exercise.

Now try this approach: Lie down, simulating sleep, and observe how the body falls naturally into steady breathing with quiet chest. Next, try to carry over the *ah-ha*-ing to a sitting position. Then comes

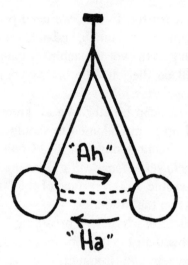

Figure 3

the real test: stand up and repeat, checking your body for surface movement.

Things to Watch For

1. *Why not breathe through the nose?* You can, of course; it's entirely natural. When speaking, we often switch from mouth breathing to nose breathing. The mouth method, however, works better, especially at the beginning, to establish control. The yawn stretch opens the throat; the sound of *ah-ha* through the mouth monitors the pendulum count; and the abdominal muscles follow through readily in support. (Note: If your mouth feels dry, stop to swallow, or take a sip of water. The dryness will taper off with continued practice.)

2. *No ballooning, please.* Be careful not to distend any area of the upper torso. Distension indicates overbreathing. Remember, you're taking in air to talk with, not to run the hundred-yard dash. The surplus air has no place to go but out—into breathy speech.

3. *Bypass the diaphragm.* Place a fist at your side just below the lower ribs to feel on inhalation the muscle expansion within. Suffice it that chest and shoulders remain uninvolved and throat unconstricted. With all quiet above the waist, the natural action below will take over.

To try, as many do, forcibly to inflate and deflate the diaphragm, a ring of muscle that moves involuntarily, means to work against your own voice. With *ah-ha* practice, try to ignore your midriff altogether (the diaphragm may remain outwardly active for a while). Concentrate on the lower regions, where the supportive action lies. Through continued trial and error, you will find that extraneous movement will decrease and disappear, however slowly.

4. *For stubborn chests and shoulders* that won't stay out of the act:

Discipline with chair. Sit on a straight-backed chair and with both hands gently grip each side underneath the seat. This directs your shoulders down, though not rigidly. With mouth dropped open, again try *ah-ha* breathing with the regular beat. Don't push your stomach out; let the breath from within move the muscles. Be patient with your body; after a while your chest movement should ease off. (See Fig. 4.)

Figure 4

Misting your mirror. As if preparing to shine the glass, breathe out in a slow, long expiration, shoulders well down. Breathe in, then out, and continue the exhaling, misting action. From the gradual loss of air, you experience a slow contraction in the girdle of breath support. Hanging on to the sensation, with hands on chest, pressing gently, begin the measured *ah-ha*'s. Have you been able to carry over that inner pulsation in the abdominal region?

Sipping through a straw. Place a straw (the ice-cream-soda kind) between your lips. With hands restraining the chest, concentrate on the gradual sucking in of air through the straw. Again that low tug in your body responds. Exhale and resume sipping air. When you've consciously located the vital area of activity, substitute the breathing routine minus the straw. Have you subdued your chest and shoulders?

Are you now in control? Suppose you can manage this passive respiration with your body responding automatically; does this mean you are in control of your breathing? Possibly, but you may be a switch-breather, like so many others. When you're silent, all goes smoothly, yet comes the moment to talk, back you switch to that unsupported breath. Once that muscle support is under control, you look, sound, and function better.

Practice makes permanent. Wherever you can, indoors or out, stay with this natural method until it takes hold. Practice even while walking. When you do, breathe through your nose, which is better equipped to filter dirt out of urban air. Remember, *no interference with the breath,* no push or extra exertion. Imagine, indeed, that you are gently drawing the breath from a deep-down well inside you. Don't get all tied up mentally; this is not an intellectual exercise. The *body* has to learn, and it will with some guidance from you. Count on extra dividends in relaxation and health.

Posture? To insist on posture control prior to breathing exercises (an old, inflexible rule) frequently inhibits what must be a relaxed approach. Some women even find it necessary to practice the *ah-ha* routine round-shouldered so as to loosen the habitual stiffness in their erect bearing.

You are lucky if you have an admirable stance and the poise that flows from it. By waiting to overcome poor posture habits, we risk losing momentum in speech improvement. When rigid rules frustrate, it's better to break them.

Tuning Up

We're ready now to place some tone on that Good Breath. Let's begin with humming, an old-time resonant aid to the voice and an unceasing pleasure.

Lips tightly together with a small space between the teeth, tip of tongue resting behind lower teeth, and jaw slack, start a humming sound, the sound of sustained *mmm.* Use a comfortable pitch without any pressure whatsoever; work for quality of tone, not volume. Most important, try to focus the hum *forward,* behind the teeth on the roof of the mouth (or hard palate), which is the sounding board for the voice.

Keep *mmm*-ing to awaken all the little-used resonating areas of head and chest. Can you sense the vibration in lips, cheekbones, under the hairline? The gentle, continuous hum soothes your throat like a massage.

Building Resonance

1. *Make waves.* Hum the pattern of three continuous waves, each growing out of the one before without pause. The pitch should rise and fall with each wave. Increase the volume gradually through the last wave. Repeat five times. Is your chest quiet, your face in repose? (See Fig. 5.)

Figure 5   THREE WAVES

2. *Sound a siren.* Imitate a distant siren resounding in a circular pattern. Your humming takes you slowly around a large circle from low note to high and back again, increasing volume and then decreasing as you close the circle. (See Fig. 6.)

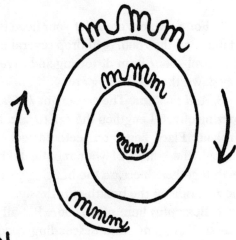

Figure 6   SIREN

Do your lips tingle? Does the resonance on the hard palate bone travel up into your head? Test by placing the palm of your hand just above your forehead to register the vibration.

3. *Hum a song,* any one that comes to mind. A chanted nursery rhyme will do. Locate and fasten in your sense memory the forward placement of humming sound. *That location above and behind your teeth is where to speak from.* Maximum clarity of speech and voice will be yours.

4. *Blend* mmm *into* ooo. "Now what *do* I *do?*" You lip round the vowel /ooo/ as in *do.* Begin with a short humming *mmm,* the resonance spilling over into the /ooo/; continue downscale from high to low in a controlled sweep. Again aware of the *behind-the-teeth* vibration, place /ooo/ forward into the same slot. Lips stay rounded as your pitch descends. (See Fig. 7.)

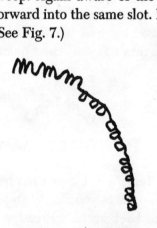

Figure 7   mmm + ooo

5. For a deeper /ooo/, let your head go until the forehead touches a table, and the /ooo/ will drop several notes. The trick is to prevent the vowel /ooo/ from distorting and to retain its *ooo*-ish sound all the way down the descending arc.

6. *Add the buzz.* The consonant /z/, as in *zeal,* produces a vibrant buzzing effect. Lengthen the /z/ to *zzzz,* as a child does when playing airplane. Place finger on teeth to feel the buzz. Direct the sound through the center of your mouth, taking care not to clamp your teeth together. Increase the buzzing sound without pressing, and let the *zzzz* ride on the breath effortlessly.

7. Buzz *plus* hum *plus* /ooo/. Put all three together, /z/ spilling into /m/ and /m/ into descending /ooo/. Take off with the Good

Breath. In blending these different sound qualities, smoothly coordinate the three shapes of teeth, tongue, and lips. For /z/, teeth meet, tongue tip is up, lips slightly parted—for /m/, tongue tip is down, lips come together—and then round for /ooo/, which descends to an effortless low pitch. (See Fig. 8.)

Figure 8   Buzz + Hum + ooo

Staying with these resonating drills will build a more vibrant voice. An ounce of resonance is worth a pound of volume. It's the difference between a fine stereo set and just a loud one.

Who's got the time? A brief pause to take up this familiar plaint before we investigate further exercise.

Cultivate the art of using your spare *and* busy time. Carrying your instrument around with you, you don't always have to shut yourself away for practice (it's no violin!). Do you manage the fifty strokes with a hairbrush? Do your humming exercise at the same time. Sitting at the desk? You can breathe rhythmically twenty-five times, and no one will be the wiser. On the telephone? Make it a practice period. And over the weekend, after the "yakkety-yakking" days, reading aloud is a creative recreation.

The daily warm-up. Awakening to a new day, welcome the attractive prospect of an enhanced speaking voice. Treat yourself to the winning combination of "fives" as you undertake these drills, already explored. They make a ten-minute package to practice and live with.

☐ For releasing built-up tensions: 5 *nods,* 5 *pillow rests,* 5 *little* and *large circles,* 5 *sighs* (p. 27);

☐ For the Good Breath: preceded by the correct progression, a series of 25 rhythmic *ah-ha's* (p. 29);

☐ **For tuning the instrument:** *humming,* 5 *waves,* 5 *sirens,* 5 *mm + ooo's,* 5 *zz + mm + ooo's* (p. 33).

The instrument has been relaxed, warmed, and tuned—and is now ready to be played. Before you do, however, a word or two about an indispensable helpmeet.

Cassette: Best Friend, Severest Critic

"Is that really me?" Comes the moment when a playback delivers a low blow to the ego. The universal reaction is shock and disbelief, even from experienced speakers. The confusion is due in part to the way we hear ourselves. Our words travel toward the ear of the listener and only indirectly to ours. An inner image of what we're saying comes to us via bone conduction in the skeletal structures above the shoulders. The recording, however, is *an accurate repro-duction of what the listener hears.*

The old addiction to habit-formed tones blurs our hearing acuity. Deflected through a protective screen, the voice image substitutes for the real thing, which we probably don't *want* to hear. Like a candid camera shot, the recording is a moment of truth.

Yes, it's really you! You can't blame your teeth, or tongue, or the machine itself (common rationales). Barring organic malfunction, we all begin with first-rate standard equipment. Excuses, remember, are designed to impress yourself first of all. Begin instead to untie the tangle of voice habits and illusion.

Look forward to a close, relaxed relationship with your cassette or tape recorder. Your ingenuity will make the most of what these mobile devices have to offer. But not right off—not until you've made progress with the breathing and voice exercises, and when you know *what* to listen for.

After the first shock has worn off and listening becomes more objective, begin to record the recommended reading-aloud routines. Work up to recording your chatting on the telephone, reading to children, or preparing interviews—an endless variety of vocal expe-riences.

But remember, self-listening can become an obsession. From time to time it is best to reverse the procedure. Place hands firmly against ears so you can't hear yourself, then speak or read and record. If you have one handy, try a wristwatch-alarm to buzz against your ear. Technically masking the voice, the opposite effect to self-hearing will transfer your attention to *feeling* what you're doing right.

Learn to listen with discrimination. More and more women are setting standards of pleasing and expressive speech. You'll find many such models to listen for and record from television and radio onto your cassette—reporters, commentators, candidates. Play and replay your favorites to recognize the specific attractive features of their voices.

Intermission for Reading Aloud

Everywhere, women in their multiform activities have begun to see the obligation of shedding slipshod, costly speech habits. But some homework is involved. Of all beneficial exercises, *reading aloud* can be one of the most pleasurable and effective means to better voice and speech.

In silent reading our eyes skim the pages; adding voice to words, we discover meanings otherwise hidden. Voice lends depth and life to language, and in turn will enrich as well the quiet reading hours. The live vibrations of poetry and prose have been recorded in printed symbols, frozen upon the page, which become sounds, then meaning, as you read aloud to yourself and to others.

As reader you are the go-between for author and listener. Communicate with direct simplicity—not as impersonally as a reporter or as emotionally involved as some actors, but as truthfully as you can. Keep foremost in mind: make the meaning clear.

The Mechanics

1. *Let your voice out.* Check with the routines for the Good Breath, also the drills to flex speech muscles and tune the instrument. Important: avoid pushing the voice into hoarseness. Learn to increase volume gradually with good abdominal support. Then pretend a hundred people make up your audience.

2. *Lead from strength.* When you strive for clarity, the main ideas should stand out in contrast to the less important ones. Instead of

playing words indiscriminately, favor those that carry the meaning, letting the others merely follow suit.

3. *Getting it together.* As you keep working for a forward flow of meaning, pull all words into line, avoiding illogical breaks between them. This linking action, so attractive to listening ears, can be profitably compared to *legato* in music, especially in song. The term means to perform without abrupt or perceptible break in movement and in a manner smooth and connected between tones or words.

4. *Naturally, record and play back.* Your cassette will help direct your practice. Until that impartial critic, the cassette, tells them so, most women cannot believe how much resonance, volume, and pauses matter for lucid expression. Don't be concerned about overdoing—underdoing is usually the main problem.

Now let's go to work. Here is a poem to enjoy by Anne Bradstreet, written, astonishingly, in 1650. From colonial days onward, our native writers and speakers have transmitted their perceptions and experiences in a continuing stream of feminine consciousness.

> I am obnoxious to each carping tongue
> Who says my hand a needle better fits;
> A poet's pen all scorn I should thus wrong,
> For such despite they cast on female wits.
> If what I do prove well, it won't advance;
> They'll say it's stol'n, or else it was by chance.
> —from *The Prologue* by Anne Bradstreet

Begin at the beginning as always with the Good Breath and use thereafter as needed. The first two lines obviously belong together. The others can be spoken singly or in combination, depending on breath and interpretation.

Techniques

1. *Lengthen the vowels* (the main word sounds) in the accented syllables and key words as marked and play down small words: *am, to, my, a* in the first two lines. Continue the rest on your own . . .

I am obnóxious to each cárping tóngue

Who sáys my hánd a néedle bétter fíts . . .

2. *Work for a smooth line* by shaping words carefully, then linking words into phrases ... "A poet's pen—all scorn—I should thus wrong ..."

3. *Increase volume gradually* toward the ends of the lines ...

"For such despite they cast on female wits."

(Note the crescendo sign ◁ which indicates a gradual increase of volume.)

The techniques make sense, as your cassette will attest. By all means proceed beyond mechanics to interpret Anne Bradstreet's poem with effects of your own.

Next, some fun with a selection, "Storyette H.M.," by Gertrude Stein (1874–1946), influential American author, famous for her salon and patronage of the arts in Paris. This sample displays her repetitious, impressionistic style.

Follow for prose the same guidelines as for poetry. "Storyette H.M." makes an excellent free-form exercise in breath control. Take off and continue as long as you can without a pause. Then, a quick breath and go on and again on, but not so fast that you lose the content since the meaning must come clear (unlikely as that might seem at first glance). Carry on with plenty of voice for this selection.

One was married to someone. That one was going away to have a good time. The one that was married to that one did not like it very well that the one to whom that one was married then was going off alone to have a good time and was leaving that one to stay at home then. The one that was going came in all glowing. The one that was going had everything he was needing to have the good time he was wanting to be having then. He came in all glowing. The one he was leaving at home to take care of the family living was not glowing. The one that was going was saying, the one that was glowing, the one that was going was saying then, I am content, you are not content, I am content, you are not content, I am content, you are content, you are content, I am content.

A play's the thing. Reading scenes from plays makes stimulating practice. The character's lines are closer to life patterns, particularly the give-and-take dialogue between people.

Watch for these "mechanics" in the upcoming selection:

1. *A comma is not a red light.* Punctuation is important mainly to the eye, not the ear. Few have the courage to bypass printed commands. To achieve more creative delivery, project meaning in thought groups (yours), adding punctuation as you see fit. The best TV commentators never sound as if they are reading, but they are—from the TelePrompTer. One major reason: their voices do not come to a halt automatically at every stop sign.

2. *The eloquent and restful pause.* A true pause is not an end but a beginning—your creative interlude between thoughts to signal something new coming up. Take adequate time to pause; as you do, you will feel the impulse to change inflection, tempo, or volume. Most readers break off too soon. Hold the pause!

3. *SOS for the sinking last word.* The All-American Drop at the end of phrases usually manages to sink the final, often indispensable word. To offset this so common fade-out, increase your energy *to* and *through* that last word. Hold on to it.

4. *Off the page.* As you develop facility, you will be able to glance ahead at the material. Contain a likely phrase in your mind, then, looking up, direct it to "those out front." Rapid and dull delivery comes from always keeping the head down with eyes riveted on print. Speaking off the page sparks your reading with eye contact, and brings a sense of immediacy to the words.

Try this speech from *Saint Joan* by George Bernard Shaw, playwright, critic, feminist. Joan, facing her inquisitors at court, discovers they intend to condemn her to life imprisonment. Joan's moving words will flow as you respond to their sounds (the feedback). For example, "You think that life is nothing but not being stone dead." Take your cue in reading aloud from lifelike patterns.

> JOAN. . . . You promised me my life; but you lied. . . . You think that life is nothing but not being stone dead. It is not the bread and water I fear; I can live on bread; when have I asked for more? It is no hardship to drink water if the water be clean. But to shut me from the light of the sky and sight of the fields

and flowers; to chain my feet, to make me breathe foul damp darkness, all this is worse than the furnace in the Bible that was heated seven times. I could drag about in a skirt; I could let the banners and the trumpets and the knights and soldiers pass me and leave me behind as they leave other women, if only I could still hear the wind in the trees, the larks in the sunshine, and the blessed, blessed church bells that send my angel voices floating to me on the wind. But without these things I cannot live; and by your wanting to take them away from me, or from any human creature, I know that your counsel is of the devil, and that mine is of God.

Especially for speech on the group plan. Reading aloud, or, as the college course is called, Oral Interpretation of Literature, despite the stuffy title, is an ideal activity for women's speech workshops. The individual reader has a ready-made audience; the group can undertake cooperative projects, particularly scenes from plays. The more ambitious can work up to a Readers' Theater, a flexible form for the presentation of a variety of literary and dramatic materials. With mere suggestions of costuming, a few props, and some reading stands, programs can achieve a professional air. The next step is the invited audience.

The dividends are obvious—voice and speech improvement, the enjoyment of literature, creative expression, and a mutual feeling of accomplishment.

3

Solutions for Common Problems

You weren't born with a speaking voice, but with the mechanism for one. If you didn't use it immediately upon entering the world, you were whacked on your bottom until you did. Speech education begins with the first birth cry. Chances are, however, that somewhere along the way we misuse the instrument with which nature handsomely endowed us.

If you belong to the fortunate great majority without organic defect in your speech and hearing machinery, you are a candidate for a good speaking voice. Most women with clear and communicative voices have had a previous history of training or experience, formal or self-directed. *A good voice is not a gift; it is an achievement.*

Is one of these lingering, hindering habits yours? Nasal tones, whispery nontones, shrill pitches, forced throaty sounds, little-girl voice with a trace of lisp, flat, nonstop monotony, hyped-up tempo and erratic rhythm, or incipient quaver (vocal wrinkles).

Lest this frank inventory frighten you off, be assured that each blemish has a remedy, though not with the advertised promise of "six easy lessons." We count on today's pressing motivations to add wings to progress. With this impetus, the straitjacket of harmful habits will come apart at the seams.

The order of study is not mandatory; if a particular exercise seems impossible, make an attempt at it, interspersed with exercises that do seem possible. Little by little, you'll find that the impossible ones become possible, and the possible become second nature. Staying with the practice routines and putting to use what you've gained matter most. Above all, don't let yourself get so wrapped up in the mechanics that you forget why you started in the first place. Keep remembering *why*.

Here are some of these most common faults—and their remedies:

Nasality, the All-American Handicap

Coast to coast, our ears are bombarded by the nasalized intonation of rock/blues/country music. Besides, our speech has some typical local features: New England twang, Midwestern flattened vowels, the Southland's strung-out nasal drawl, the West's heavier TV-type variant of Amurrican "nosiness." Can these unattractive sounds be channeled through the mouth instead? Of course, but, again, it takes some doing.

Am I Really Nasal? Test yourself with a cassette or tape recorder (or ask your best friend). A simple do-it-yourself test: hold your nose and speak separately the long sounds *ah, ee, ay, eye, oh*. If your nose vibrates on one or more, you probably do have some nasality. Or you may have a metallic tone that closely resembles a nasal one, commonly brought on by taut throat muscles imprisoning the voice back of the tongue.

> If *to do* were as easy
> as to *know* what were *good* to do,
> chapels had been churches
> and poor men's cottages princes' palaces.
> Portia, *The Merchant of Venice*

Remedies (preceded always by the Good Breath)

1. *Letting the air in.* Begin by yawning. With mouth open, hold your jaw down firmly with your hand to prevent its snapping all the way back after the stretch. Read aloud Portia's lines (above) with lips held apart the width of two fingers. The lips will need to come together briefly for some of the consonants but otherwise stay open, your hand gently urging the jaw to unlock. If the tight muscles between chin and ear begin to ache, massage them softly and the ache will taper off.

2. *The cork bit.* Trim a cork down to about a nickel's size but half an inch thick. Place it between your teeth and talk or read, lips

protruding, in this rather uncomfortable position. Never mind, for this too will persuade a set mouth to unclamp. Then remove the cork and, holding it in front of your mouth, imagine it's still there between the teeth. Oddly, you develop a sense of openness behind the lips and a softer jawline. Do you already notice that your tone has somewhat altered?

3. *Speaking over a yawn.* Localized tension in the voice zone and nasal tones often go together. Once again yawn, but this time as the cheeks stretch, begin sighing the words, "If to do were as easy as to know what were good to do . . . etc." Don't be thrown by the foggy effect (like a hushed "mike voice"), strangely as it may strike your ears.

As this let-go sensation of sighed tone, backed with chest resonance, shakes loose an old habit, the nasal tone will vanish in the fog. After that you diminish the breathiness (and the phoniness), retaining the open-throated soft attack, an antidote to even a touch of nasality.

4. *Isolating the troublemakers.* One of the more successful cures consists of singling out the vowel sounds you now channel through your nose and learning how to reroute them through your mouth. A later section on vowels (p. 62) gives you detailed directions on how to go about accomplishing this. Before undertaking that job, begin a successful offensive by concentrating on the voice treatments to combat nasality.

Reminder: Your daily humming exercises will sensitize you to what *correct* nasal resonance feels like—to be expended only on consonants /m/, /n/, /ng/, and never on vowels.

Those Inadequate Tones: "What did you say?"

To be heard and understood are two sides of the same coin, the simple basic goals of spoken exchange. How often a woman's contribution gets lost around a conference table, and, actually, how antisocial it is to keep ears straining. Inaudible voices no longer suit today's life and work styles. There is no personality change so telling as the voice which at last can be comfortably, not just barely, heard.

Remedies

1. *Speak out front.* Use a small megaphone, or make one out of paper. Direct your words through the cone, a primitive gimmick to focus the voice outward where it belongs and to prompt you to open up.

2. *The pencil mike.* Have you observed how skillfully newscasters on TV employ mikes in interviews? Hold an ordinary pencil about eight inches from your lips and speak toward the point. Your purpose is the same as with the megaphone, to draw your voice out, pointing it at the mike. As your tones amplify, improvise a short speech directed at your "audience." The cassette will corroborate the improvement.

3. *Building your voice from the bottom up.* Back to fundamentals and the Good Breath. A *quick test:* with hand on abdomen, exclaim as if warning someone, "Watch out!" Do you feel your hand being pulled back? (Even the smallest voice will open up on *"FIRE!"*

Once again to continue building strength: hands on abdomen, take a good breath, then hands pressing in, call out "Yoh!" Do the muscles bounce against your hand? Persevere with this simple drill: *breath—hands—*"Yoh!"—until the muscles respond and you experience this new coordination of expansion and contraction on voice.

4. *Progress to phrases.* Combine the same hand action and body reaction with these phrases: *"Let's Go!" "Quiet down, please!"* and other commands. *Warning:* avoid pressuring to increase volume or the throat will rebel with hoarseness and pain. Stay loose. If your pitch rises sharply, you're sure to be straining. As you build correct bodily reinforcement, the voice will grow stronger naturally.

5. *The pelvic pull.* Coordinated properly, this exercise is very effective. Standing, place hands firmly, palms down, on the back of a couch or armchair. Stationing hands right there, step back from them as far as you can go until your arms straighten and you feel a tugging in the pelvic region. Your back is now parallel with head in line, and legs perpendicular to the floor. Shoulders should remain relaxed and throat free throughout the exercise. (See Fig. 9.)

In that position, count aloud from one to ten, taking a breath (with jaw slack) before each number. Feel the pelvic pull like a reflex:

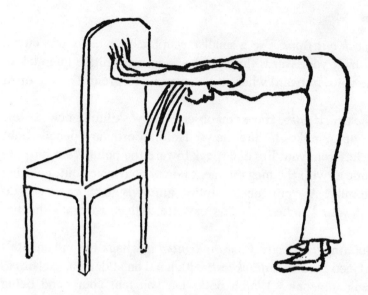

Figure 9

breath→"one"→reflex; breath→"two"→reflex; breath→and so on. The numbers resound ever more clearly as you progress to ten.

Walking slowly back to where your hands are, *count down* from "ten" to "one" (always the Good Breath precedes the number). When you reach "one," your body has gradually straightened and you are upright. Standing at ease, repeat several times, *"one, one, one"*; the repetition of "one" cues you in each time to *breath, voice + reflex.* Now, making good use of this technique, test your carrying power on a short poem. (The slashes tell you where to pause briefly for a breath.)

> / Give me your tired, / your poor,
> Your huddled masses / yearning to breathe free
> / The wretched refuse of your teeming shore
> / Send these / the homeless, tempest-tossed, to me:
> / I lift my lamp beside the golden door.
> —Emma Lazarus (1849–87)

Speak up, imagining a forty-foot living room. After each slash, read aloud with a resounding "one"—like this:

(Breath) "one" Give me your tired,
(Breath) "one" your poor, your huddled masses
(Breath) "one" yearning to breathe free.

Next, carry on without "one." Just take a breath as indicated and continue reading with sustained strength. In a circular process, the feedback of your own enriched sounds deepens your response to the poetry itself. The cassette will surprise you.

From Poetry to Ordinary. Carry over your new-found vocal energy from the poem to everyday speech: *"The meeting is adjourned," "Is anybody home?" "Taxi!"* Good tone breeds more good tone, renewing itself constantly, improving with use. You'll make the discovery that it is easier to talk with full tone than with that still, small voice, composed mainly of unvoiced air.

Pressure-cooker Speech

Huskiness, harshness, hoarseness: we lump these terms together to describe pushing-from-the-throat voice production. Time was when such pressure-cooker speech was mostly male. But of late, more and more women have fallen into the trap of confusing forceful personality with vocal force.

Shrillness and stridency, pressuring the pitch upward, have long been with us. In either case, whether low and gravelly or high and shrieky, such voices are hard on speakers' throats and listeners' ears.

You can apply wrong forces anywhere in the speech mechanism: constriction in low and high throat areas, stiffness in tongue and lips, and tightness in the jaw. For this constant war on vocal cords, the penalty is likely to be recurrent bouts with laryngitis. In addition, extreme pushiness can be seen as well as heard: veins on the neck stand out as faces flush with effort—all told, an unflattering cosmetic effect.

Remedies

1. *Five Areas of Release*
—*Massage the face and throat.* Let the hands slide from the hairline down the cheeks until the jaw sags. If this lends you a silly look,

that's fine—you're letting go. Stroke the throat with weightless fingertips.

—*Thrust out the tongue.* A most unbecoming means to a good end: stick your tongue out, letting it flop on the lower lip. Don't shove. Go for at least five tongue-flops.

—*Ease the jaw.* With hands on both sides of the chin, move the jaw from *side to side.* Let your hands do it: working that hard bone from inside will only add tension. Next, chin in hands, your fingers guide the jaw *up and down.* Keep at it and the resistance will give way.

—*Soften the swallowing muscles.* When you swallow, discover the small muscles moving under your fingers beneath the jawbone. Massage them with both hands in soothing rotary motion until the tissues feel soft.

—*Loosen the back of the neck.* Raise your head up and let it fall, up and down in a silent "Yes—yes—yes." Then slow motion from side to side, "No, no, no." Repeat a series of "yesses" and "noes" until the neck and the rest of the speech musculature is in respose.

This overall massage sequence will bring relief to aching neck tensions and, of course, especially to driven voices. *Take as directed* (frequently).

2. *With the greatest of ease.* Don't wait for your day to begin; start breathing exercises in bed. Already familiar with our *ah-ha*-ing method (pp. 29 to 31), try this beneficial variation:

Remove the pillow from under your head. Lie in a restful position with knees bent and feet flat on the bed. Yawn (so easy in bed), and as the throat stretches, slowly breathe *out* (for you, out is important). Take this one-to-five count for a breathing drill: *short* inhale (count 1); *long* exhale (count 5) in that order. Repeat at least ten times. Below, the low muscles continue their supportive action; above the waistline, all is quiet. (Of course, count silently.)

3. *Some gentle traction for neck tension.* Still in bed, with arms overhead, tuck your hands into the space between headboard and mattress. Hold them there firmly. Without raising your head and with arms pulling gently backward, press the back of your head into the mattress. Move head halfway to the right and press in again; turn all the way to the right and press. Return to center and perform the same three presses to the left. Repeat. (See Fig. 10.)

Ready to rise, roll over to the side of the bed. Sitting on the edge,

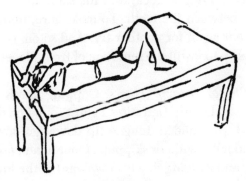

Figure 10

straighten back and rotate head slowly, stopping at the center as you go; change directions and add some soft humming. You've soothed the way to another day.

4. *The match trick.* Do you think, perhaps, that the vocal cords are the source of power? They are not; the breath (technically, the *activator*) is. Words rammed through the cords will jam in the throat. A slogan to paste on your mirror: *Don't make it happen, let it happen.*

An ordinary kitchen match, if deftly handled, can coax trapped tones forward. Place the match lightly between the teeth, front and center. Don't clamp down. Hold the end just firmly enough to stay in the mouth. Try to speak normally as if the match weren't there at all. Talk on, even on the telephone, focusing your tone toward the blue or red tip (the person on the other end will never notice).

Some familiar lines from "The Battle Hymn of the Republic" by Julia Ward Howe (1819–1910) to practice on:

/ Mine eyes have seen the glory of the coming of the Lord:
/ He is trampling out the vintage / where the grapes of wrath are
        stored:
/ He hath loosed the fateful lightning / of his terrible swift sword:
/ His truth is marching on.

Match between teeth, *read aloud toward the tip*, taking breaths as marked. Careful not to set your jaw. Note that besides focusing the voice outward, the match helps you link the words smoothly.

After finishing the stanza, remove the match. Hold it close to your mouth and repeat, trying to recapture the same forward impulse as with the match between the teeth. To make sure, reinsert for more practice. Then out again for another try. And so on. Remember, the match is just a prop to instill the sensation of front placement for your voice.

5. *Light drills for "heavy" voices.* Cupping hands around your mouth, take an easy breath. Imitating a ghost sound on the wind, call *hooo-hooooooo.* Lips rounded, tongue tip down, go downscale from high to low, gradually, without skipping. Once again, *hooo-hooooooo,* reaching higher and winding slowly downward to the lowest register. Perform this light-as-air pattern over and over, the sound growing freer, like an echo.

6. *Now enjoy this.* On different pitch levels, playfully toss off *Hoo—hee—hay—hi—ho.* The sounds seem to bounce at random from high to low to middle and back again. Take sips of air between. A voice can lose most of its gravel with this one.

7. *A different hum. Hn—hn.* With the tip of tongue behind the teeth for the sound of /n/, combine /n/ with /h/. Hold on to the *nnnn,* a soft moaning, humming sound. Let your head go around as you *hnnnn-hnnnn-hnnnn* ever so lightly. Take a breath each time.

Recommended for pressurized speech. For the rough-textured tone, usually considered masculine (well, maybe on men it sounds good), practice diligently the technique of speaking over a yawn (p. 43). This sighed approach (somewhat fashionable) cuts down constriction in jaw and throat. While you certainly can't yawn at people, the remembered sensations from your practice will encourage a softer attack.

For the daily rounds. Before uttering a word, make sure the area under the chin is free. Start all conversation with a mild *outgoing* breath. This takes the load of air off your chest. It may be hard on your glands to discipline yourself to a vocal slowdown, but what a fine antidote for what ails you! Do you seem to be uncomfortably dragging your words? Let friend cassette convince you how much better you sound to others.

Remember: all change appears even painfully uncomfortable at first. If it weren't, you'd have cause for worry since you wouldn't be improving anything.

The Little-girl Voice

Quite suddenly during puberty, a girl's vocal cords grow a vital eighth of an inch, lowering her pitch by two or three notes. Not as spectacular as her brother's voice change (his drops an octave), hers attracts little attention. Resisting the natural drop, she may cling to a little-girl voice. Arrested at a twelve-year age level, such childish tones will persist into adulthood even though adolescent emotional conflicts have long been forgotten. Remember, every voice has a lower pitch lurking in its range—you need only uncover it.

Remedies

1. *Put your body behind it.* Are you speaking with only the top layer of a seven-layer structure? Activating the other layers can bring your climbing pitch down to earth. Seek the solution in the Good Breath, and associated exercises (p. 28). To step up corrective action, add this: breathe all the way out as far as you can go, then, practically airless, count down aloud "Five-four-three-two-one," linking the numbers. At this point (number 1) be aware of that low tug along with a significantly lowered pitch.

Continue with the long exhale and the countdown until the routine pays off in the firmer control of a new, conditioned reflex. A slogan to paste on your mirror: *"Tone—not air!"* Little-girl voices are breathy, an unattractive feature.

2. *Bring your pitch down . . . down.* This can be tricky, but great if it works, and it should, eventually. Cover ears with hands to block any interfering noise and hum up- and downscale. At the place where the hum reverberates the loudest in your head, you can determine your natural pitch.

Follow the same routine, repeating the word "so" up and down the spoken scale, until you discover the place where "so" resounds the most. At that spot say, "So, this sounds pretty good to me!" Of course, at this point, reach for your cassette. Have you arrived at your optimum pitch? Undoubtedly, it's at least three notes lower than your habitual one. (Of course, this method can work as well for raising pitches.)

3. *Psychological aid. Think* lower by keeping hand on chest

(perhaps fingering your necklace) while you speak. This elementary gimmick can work like a charm to bring down a soaring pitch. See how low you can *think!*

4. *Sample the grunt-and-groan school.* "*Oh my, it's going to rain.*" Declare in a groaning voice, elongating the key vowels. As you go on grunting and groaning other complaints, listen intently to that low register. (Is it really yours?) Since one groans not from the head but from the belly, become sensitized to the accompanying pull in that region.

5. *Sing and say.* Are you one of the lucky ones with a pleasant singing voice—or maybe you're just a contented bathtub warbler? Quite commonly, thin, high speaking voices become lower-keyed and fuller in song. In our myriad American choirs, choruses, and glee clubs, we sing better than we speak. Perhaps this is because song has pleasurable associations while our spoken words too often reflect pressures in mind and body.

The technique: Don't be shy. Improvise a melody (anything that comes to mind) to sing to these lines of poetry; then speak them. *Sing a line, say the line.*

> Sing: Tyger! Tyger! burning bright
> Say: Tyger! Tyger! burning bright
> Sing: In the forests of the night . . .
> Say: ditto

Observe how melody carries tone forward without breaks between these splendid lines by William Blake. When you *sing,* how delightful that resonance, a more relaxed pitch, and smoother phrasing will spill over into the *speaking* of them. Now, try these excerpts:

> She walks in beauty, like the night
> Of cloudless climes and starry skies . . .
> —Lord Byron

> The Moving Finger writes; and, having writ,
> Moves on . . .
> —Edward Fitzgerald (*Omar Khayyam*)

If you are given to spontaneous singing of snatches of song, by all means put them to work in song-to-speech practice. If this technique doesn't work automatically, a little persistence will reward you. Many have sung their way to better speech. Besides, it's fun.

6. *Stabilize the pitch—read to the floor.* Sit in a comfortable chair and place book on the floor. Let go from the waist, rag-doll fashion, head between your legs; read aloud in this position, placing the cassette at your feet. Retain the overall released feeling; straightening up, read on. Play back the tape, and hear (to your surprise) a more sonorous pitch, closer to the bottom reaches of your voice. It may sound strange, but who cares? (See Fig. 11.)

Figure 11

7. *Play the pitch pipe /ooo/.* To warm up for this one, work the drill of vibrant *mmm* flowing into descending /ooo/ (p. 34). With the Good Breath ahead, hum the *mmm* and, rounding your lips, take /ooo/ downscale as far as you can go comfortably. Have you uncovered the low /ooo/ hiding somewhere in the natural range of your voice? Ready now to undertake the pitch pipe, a shortened *mmmooo* cut down from the original drill.

The *mmmooo*, a valuable aid, will key you into these opening lines from Genesis. After a breath at the slash mark, intone *mmmooo* on your low pitch, then attach it smoothly to the first word of every phrase.

/ *mmmooo* In the beginning God created the heaven and the earth
/ *mmmooo* And the earth was without form and void
/ *mmmooo* And darkness was upon the face of the deep

/*mmmooo* And the spirit of God moved upon the face of the waters

/ *mmmooo* And God said let there be light and there was light.

Did you sustain the pitch from word to word with increasing volume to the end of the phrase? If the unaccustomed pitch wavers, stop anywhere in your reading; have another go at the pitch pipe *mmmooo* and carry on to finish the phrase.

Repeat the biblical excerpt, this time placing your hand just below the collarbone. Can you pick up the growing hum there as you increase the volume? Your vibrators (head, body bones, and cavities above and below the voice box), these built-in amplifiers, supply you with carrying power. Reinforce by stopping during the reading to interject some automatic remarks with that pleasant pitch. *"What's your name?" "Please shut the door."*

8. *Practice out loud.* Give your all. (*Let* the neighbors complain!) None of this happens automatically. Remember how long you've been living with that high-pitched delivery. If you hang on, your body will direct you to that pleasant register. One day comes the discovery that this warm, matured manner of speaking is in the true sense your natural voice. And you will decide to live happily with it forever after.

A Mixed Bag: Monotony, Hyped-up Tempo, Erratic Rhythms

1. *Sameness and grayness.* Monotony is a common fault, visual as well as vocal when dead-level sounds issue from deadpan faces. The most significant words lose color and impact with such delivery.

2. *How fast should you talk?* At the rate at which you can be understood readily. Hurried speech is as antisocial as the kind that can't be heard; both strain the listener's attention and transmit inner tensions. Excessive speed never leaves enough time for good tone. Letting up lends you pace and space for improvement; hearing yourself better, you help yourself speak better.

3. *Communication disorder.* Big-city, jerky rhythms agitate the sound waves that conduct the traffic of spoken language. Daily talk in speeded-up staccato, with arbitrary stops piled on careless articulation, cut down vital person-to-person exchange. Include, too, that

All-American *drop* at the end of phrases, which usually loses the last, often indispensable word.

Remedies

A *three-way deal* for talk, monotonous, fast, or choppy: directed reading-aloud routines expressly designed for each. Three short selections from Emily Dickinson (1830–86) provide the exercise material. With Dickinson for practice, even drilling can be fulfilling.

1. *Monotony.* Joanie-One-Notes give little audio pleasure. Exercise for flexibility breaks up dull, congealed patterns. Have the courage to ride over the rut of habit. Follow the directions for voice changes, mechanically, without self-consciousness. Observe the slash marks for breath.

A Narrow Fellow in the Grass

(SLOWER) / A narrow fellow in the grass occasionally
rides; (FASTER) / You may have met him—did you not?
/ His notice sudden is. (SOFTER) / The grass divides
as with a comb, a spotted shaft is seen; (LOUDER)
/ And then it closes at your feet and opens farther
on. (HIGHER) / Several of nature's people I know,
and they know me; (LOWER) / I feel for them a transport of cordiality. (Now all three at once: FASTER,
LOUDER, HIGHER) / But never met this fellow, attended
or alone. (SLOWER, SOFTER, LOWER) / Without a tighter
breathing, / And zero at the bone.

2. *Runaway speed.* Slowing down alone is not the answer. Adding one word to the next like linked sausages has a deadening effect. To slow your reading down without sounding labored, and to bring clarity to delivery, hang on to the main sounds (especially the leading vowels) of all key words in the poem. Another deterrent to hurrying is to stretch your pause at ends of phrases before you take a breath at the next slash mark.

I Never Saw

/ I *never saw* a *moor,* (PAUSE) / I *never saw* the *sea;*
(PAUSE) / Yet *know* I *how* the *heather looks,* And

what a *wave* must *be*. (PAUSE) / I *never* spoke with
God, Nor *visited* in *heaven*; (PAUSE) / Yet *certain*
am I of the *spot* (PAUSE) / As if the *chart* were *given*.

3. *Contagious, erratic rhythms*. Our ears sop up the scrambled, enveloping beat; as we speak, we infect each other, causing mutual unease. For English to be truly communicative, we must connect words into phrases in a flow of sound and sense.

In the poem, the key sounds are underlined and words joined. Proceeding slowly, learn the linking sensation of the next sound being formed *before* the previous one is completed. Work for an unbroken continuity until you reach the slash marks, where you pause to take a breath.

Presentiment

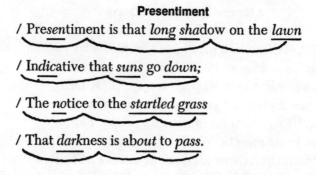

/ Presentiment is that *long shadow* on the *lawn*

/ Indicative that *suns* go *down*;

/ The *notice* to the *startled grass*

/ That *darkness* is about to *pass*.

4

Speaking Good United States

American English came of age long ago as a written and spoken language. Its intrinsic sounds are as beautiful and effective as any English anywhere and, like a rich mother lode, it is ours for the digging.

Some of us sit for hours, presumably for relaxation, pouring brain energy into some word game. Yet no fun with words or treasure hunt can match the excitement of exploring the vigor and variety in our native tongue. Along with improved clarity of voice and speech, women need to form a more personal, deep-going attachment to the language, seeking in its munificent supply the words to choose and use—words to live with.

What is good American speech? It is a means of *national* communication, *contemporary* and free of conspicuous localisms and affectation, readily *understandable*—and all in good voice.

No section of the country has a monopoly on good or bad speech. Though Brooklynese gets the most laughs, voices of engaging quality (and the reverse) can be heard in that borough as they can in Memphis or Tulsa or Houston.

Unlike some European countries, we have no official guardians of correct usage; nor, as in more class-conscious England, is the language stratified according to rank and station. Aspiring American women of varying backgrounds can acquire clear "classless" speech by study and application.

Who are the models? An American speech standard does exist, one that has proven itself with audiences across the land. National television and radio announcers, newscasters, and commentators can generally be counted upon to use the language sensitively and well.

Their standard exemplifies a truly composite style which, while basically Middle Western, is modified by the speech patterns of other areas. Now risen above the old recipe bit, women as reporters, interviewers, and panelists are meeting the media's challenge with impressive clarity of voice and words. Actresses and popular singers with skilled articulation also make good models.

Unity in variety. People the world over claim they can always spot someone "from the States." Obviously then, from coast to coast, similarities in our speech outweigh differences. But even as the leveling process goes on, we continue to flavor our talk with local color. No one would mistake a New York telephone operator for her Vermont counterpart or a Philadelphia congresswoman for one from Boston. And wouldn't the lady from Texas bristle if anyone mistook her for a Georgian—and vice versa, of course?

Anything goes? While we may have the liberty to speak as we wish, do we therefore have the license to drag the language down? It is the fashion among some authorities to maintain that comprehension is all. True enough, slangy, slurred usage can make itself perfectly clear—"Watchadoin" . . . "Seeinya" . . . "Zatso" . . . "Yawl." But these slovenly contractions "jest ain't" good speech!

Formally we say, "I shall not speak"; informally, "I won't speak." We all know, however, that "I ain't gonna say nothin' " is beyond the pale. We can steer a course between stuffiness and sloppiness.

Our leaders render a disservice when they talk down in a folksy one-of-the-boys manner. Women in leadership should not ape this practice by embracing cozy vernacular, which really just comes down to an easy out. Localisms may be vivid and even enriching, but take care that this comfortable chatter communicates beyond the immediate area. Remember that good American speech should have *national* relevance in today's communication.

Let us examine an attractive facet of our language that suffers from general neglect. When put to good use, we will have another tool for upgrading the spoken word.

The Built-in Beat

"I'm going for a *long walk*," she an*nounced* non*chalant*ly. The genius of our mother tongue lies in the vivid contrasts between strong and weak word types, and between divisions within those words called syllables.

English is described as a *stress* language (a technical, not an emotional term) because its stresses, or accents, are sharper than in many other languages. Unaware of their unique character, we use these accents quite naturally in our talk. But do we use them effectively? If so, all our speaking would be enlivened by this built-in beat transmitting lucid signals of meaning to listeners. *Learn how to stay with the beat!*

The telegram test. "Since my daughter has been hospitalized for an appendectomy, I regret that it is impossible for me to attend tomorrow's meeting of the League of Women Voters at five o'clock." How unlikely that anyone (even the very rich) would send such a wire. The message would probably read:

DAUGHTER HOSPITALIZED CANNOT ATTEND MEETING SORRY

When sending a telegram, we have little difficulty in selecting the key words to convey our message. Inevitably the choice is from the strong word types: nouns, active verbs, and often adjectives and adverbs. So with speaking. By featuring the essential words and underplaying unimportant ones, we save energy and deliver the meaning.

Here are two lines of a stanza from "Often Rebuked," a poem by Emily Brontë (1818–48). See if you can reduce her key words to a telegram.

> I'll walk where my own nature would be leading—
> It vexes me to choose another guide—

In the flow of speech, words gain or lose importance by contrast. An overemphatic woman hammering at each word loses us; we follow her only with difficulty, for if everything is accentuated, nothing is.

Light and shade produce the telling rhythms that capture our attention as illustrated in this advertiser's slogan:

Never underestimate the *power* of a *woman.*

Should you wish to place extra emphasis on the negative word "never," double its stress: *Never* underestimate, etc. Or perhaps you'd prefer to underscore the word *power* or *woman.* Emphasis is your choice. It can take many forms depending upon what you want to express beyond the natural accents which are inherent in English structure:

The Big Four (nouns, verbs, adjectives, and *adverbs)* always carry the main burden of our meaning. Their number forever expands, fattening the already bulging stock of dynamic language in our dictionaries.

The connectives, small words, only one hundred or so but repeated endlessly, have mainly a connective function. Do you mistakenly accent the weak word types, throwing out of kilter meaning and rhythm? Like this: "I want *to* think about *it.*" Watch "of," "to," "in," "at," "with," and all the other little prepositions that load our speech. Likewise the ever-recurring *ands* should not be hit; a conjunction is a mere joiner of words. "*And* we went to the country *and* met some friends *and* went swimming *and . . .*" is a boring routine.

The articles, weakest of words (*a, an, the*), will catch you if you don't watch out. Avoid blowing up *a* by pronouncing it *ay,* a long attention-getting sound, instead of the neutral and unobtrusive *uh.* Politicos usually go overboard on this as they proclaim "I give you *ay man who . . . ,*" but they aren't the only guilty ones. Much daily talk is punctuated by this destroyer of speech cadence. "Ay (uh) girl of twelve is not ay (uh) child." Remember it's *an* before a vowel: *a friend* but *an enemy;* note also the *(thuh) theater* and the *(thee) opera.*

She, it, they, his and the rest of the *pronouns* tend to ensnare us. Especially the most personal of all, *I,* should be soft-pedaled. Used overmuch, it smacks of self-importance; with added vocal push, the damage multiplies. "*I* said to her," "*I* thought," *I . . . I . . . I. . . .* How tiresome can you get?

Weak but not slurred. Do not confuse essential weakening with the slipshod habit of slurring. *Unstressing,* an earmark of English, performs as importantly in making good sense as *stressing.* It is contrast, the small words contributing their weak beat, that makes the relationship or words clear to the listener. Read aloud the short poem "L'Envoi" by Dorothy Parker (1896–1967). Tone down the crossed-out words.

> ~~Oh~~, beggar ~~or~~ prince, no more, no more!
> Be off ~~and~~ away ~~with~~ your strut ~~and~~ show.
> ~~The~~ sweeter ~~the~~ apple, ~~the~~ blacker ~~the~~ core—
> Scratch ~~a~~ lover, ~~and~~ find ~~a~~ foe!

Rhythms within *words.* Probably the most distinctive feature of English pronunciation is the richly varied accents within words of more than one syllable. The leading syllable, which can occur anywhere in a word, becomes its accented peak, the lesser ones becoming correspondingly weaker: HAPPiness, deMOCracy, motiVAtion. Thus we steal from one segment of a word to empower another: əMERican, MELədy, əTHORəty. (That little symbol for *uh* is called *schwa.*)

The variety of word rhythms. Read these words aloud. They embody the six most common syllable patterns. Remember to keep the main sound (always one vowel sound) long and clear.

1. WOman, SPEAKing, MOVEment (strong-weak, the most common accent pattern)
2. sucCESS, aWARE, reCRUITS (weak-strong)
3. BEAUtiful, AGitate, LIBerate (strong-weak-weak)
4. underSTAND, perseVERE, interRUPT (weak-weak-strong)
5. proFESsion, aMENDment, eLECtion (weak-strong-weak)
6. BREAKTHROUGH, MOONLIGHT, HODGEPODGE (strong-strong, the least common)

Don't strike at sounds for emphasis; that will make words jump out at people. To bring out the underlying beat, just *lean* on the key syllables, elongating the vowel within. Reduce the others proportionately to achieve balance. Pulsation and clarity will permeate your conversation.

Now all together. Read aloud this excerpt from Walt Whitman. Stay with the rhythm throughout as you follow the markings (/) for the strong beat and (ᵕ) for the weak.

/ ᵕ ᵕ / ᵕ / ᵕ ᵕ / ᵕ ᵕ
Language is not an abstract construction of

ᵕ / ᵕ ᵕ / ᵕ ᵕ / ᵕ   ᵕ /
the learned, or of dictionary makers . . . and has

ᵕ / ᵕ / ᵕ / / ᵕ ᵕ /
its bases broad and low, close to the ground.

With this basic method of marking, do you feel the inner pulse beneath the words as you speak them? Why not try this approach when reading aloud.

These patterns of strong and weak accents, heard in continuity, make good sense at the listening end. Consciously apply the built-in beat of the rhythms of English and, like the steps of a familiar dance, they will become second nature.

The Sounds and Shapes of American English

"Open your mouth and say *ah*," quotes the doctor—that's a *vowel*. Sneeze and you hear, "Tch, tch!" or hush someone and your lips form, "Sh, sh"—those are *consonants*. When you open your mouth, *keeping the tip of the tongue at the bottom*, and then voice an *unobstructed* breath, you form a vowel *(oh, ooh, ow*, etc.); add a consonant and Wow! By shaping the breath and articulating with tongue, teeth, and lips, you have a consonant *(m, t, v, l)*.

Vowels

Ear, not eye. Ask anyone to name the vowels and the wrong answer usually comes, "*a, e, i, o, u*." These are *letters* (visual concepts), not *sounds*. American English has sixteen basic *spoken* vowels (see pp. 66 ff. for "vowel wheels").

The glamorous vowel. From the day a singer stands up to a piano, she begins and continues to vocalize on vowels, the main vehicle of voice. Shortening these sounds, a common practice, means cutting off your tone to spite your voice. Look at a bit of Shakespeare with squashed vowels. Imagine how it *sounds!*

> Say you that I one day may be fitted with a husband?
> Not till God make men of some other metal than earth.
> —Beatrice in *Much Ado about Nothing*

At the other extreme, Southern and Western drawlers of vowels stretch and *strehihtch* them into distortion.

Whether you say *Flahrida* or *Flawrida, daughter* or *dotter, horrible* or *hawrible, further* or *fuhthuh, awfice* or *ahffice (not aw-uhfiss), eyether* or *eether,* should occasion no argument. *Bahth* for *bath* sounds affected but not in *Bahston,* where it is "standard." The same is true for *I*'s that sound more like *aah*'s in the Southland.

None of us is free from sectional sounds, nor should we want to be; distracting localisms, however, should be screened out of talk if you want people to listen to *what* you say. Heard much too often: *po-lees* (police), *ree-ceive, beauteeful, Dee-troit,* and so on and on. *Don't flatten your rhythms. Stay with the beat!*

Motivated listening. Even houses in remote hamlets reveal on their roofs that TV link with "civilization." In the speech flooding the airwaves, fasten your eyes and ears on national news and talk shows from which your vowels should not stray too far. Really tune in as you turn on your set; listen and learn.

A vowelizing routine for practice

> Let husbands know
> Their wives have sense like them. They see, and smell,
> And have their palates both for sweet and sour,
> As husbands have . . .
> —Emilia in *Othello*

1. Write the first line on a piece of paper.

2. Now underline the main vowels.

     Let husbands know their wives have sense like them.

3. Next, extract all the vowels and connect them with loops, like this:

     eh uh oh eye aa eh eh

4. Cassette at hand, clearly voice this vowel chain without stops between them. As you play back, hear as well as feel a tonal continuity.

5. Now replacing the consonants, speak the whole sentence:

Let husbands know their wives have sense like them.

Link all sounds with the consonants bridging the vowels. Play it back. Hear how much clearer the vowels sound now. Repeat the removing-and-replacing technique on the rest of the excerpt.

Try this vowelizing on some improvised conversation. "Th*a*nk y*ou* for an enj*oy*able *e*vening. In " 'Bye now," isolating the vowels you get "eye-ow, eye-ow." Replace the consonants and the pearshaped tones fairly sing!

Round your lips for the round shapes. Feel and hear how, in this excerpt, the main vowel sounds are reinforced by your lip-rounding:

> Beautiful for situation,
> the joy of the whole earth is Mount Zion . . .
> —Psalm XLVIII

Some Prescriptions for Ailing Vowels

1. *It's Number One.* The nasal *a* as in *may-un* ("man") has been dubbed the "American" vowel. No respecter of state boundaries, it should perhaps be declared a national disaster. This twang (*twayng*), so much with us, scars countless words:

ayund (and)	*ayngry* (angry)	*maynage* (manage)
sayng (sang)	*payunts* (pants)	*haym* (ham)

and also infects words (without *n, m* or *ng*) like:

layst (last)	*ayfter* (after)	*glayss* (glass)

Let's see if we can undo some of the damage to this fine English vowel.

Make the nose test. Hold your nostrils lightly and pronounce "ran" in slow motion, r-a-n. You should feel no buzz on /r/ or /a/ but a noseful on /n/. Should you also feel a reaction on /r/ and /a/, you have some work to do.

A good denasalizer. Releasing your jaw and holding your tongue down with the back of a spoon, you can hardly help producing an unblemished /a/. Beginning as usual with the Good Breath, keep mouth untensed, the tongue lying flat at the bottom, and have a go at these words: d*a*nce, *a*nguish, b*a*nk, m*a*nner.

Now reverse this correct procedure by raising the tip of the tongue and curling it back. Do you feel and hear a bleat where the good vowel should be? This is what's known as *negative* practice to achieve *positive* results.

As a reward, you can take on these words of Marianne Moore (from the poem "Poetry") for practice. Remember tongue down, mouth relaxed on the /ă/s in the *underlined* words.

> . . . if you *demand* on the one *hand,*
> the raw material of poetry in
> all its rawness *and*
> that which is on the other *hand*
> genuine, then you are interested in poetry.

2. *The cat's meow.* The /ow/ rates as the number two offender in the land. Do you go *day-oon tay-oon* to shop *downtown?* Mostly this happens when /ow/ is followed by /n/ as in "sound," "round," "bound," and "downtown."

The cure. *Ah* and *oo* are involved this time, blended into a diphthong—a single compound vowel /ow/. Always think *ah*, first opening your relaxed mouth to accommodate *ah*'s size. Then follow through with a short lip-rounded *oo* to pronounce /ow/—and you'll *not* route the sound through your nose.

Detach the sound /ow/ from the contagious *n* and repeat (remember, the tongue tip stays down for all /ow/'s).

> doubt-doubt-dah-oo-n-(down)
> crowd-crowd-crah-oo-n-(crown)
> mouth-mouth-mah-oo-nd-(mound)

Next, a bit of Hamlet's famous advice to the players. Pull the words together as you speak them, making certain that no nasality creeps into the *underlined* /ow/ words.

Speak the speech, I pray you, as I *pronounc'd* it to you, trip-pingly on the tongue; but if you *mouthe* it, as many of your players do, I had as lief the *town*-crier spoke my lines.

3. *Other "nosy" sounds.* Let's face it, we habitually nasalize other vowels too, though less frequently than /ă/ or /ow/. When in doubt, try the nose test, and if you detect other twangy sounds, follow the same prescriptions. For example:

> tie-tie-t-eye-m-(time)
> say-say-say-m-(same)
> tea-tea-t-ee-m-(team)

Invent your own drills; they're often the best kind (keye-nd).

The word *time* crops up constantly, and often takes a beating. It is either nasalized or dropped back into the throat to sound closer to *t-oy-m* than *t-eye-m*. Again the tongue is literally at the bottom of it all. Some more brief Shakespeare for practice:

> Men have died from *time* to *time*
> and worms have eaten them,
> but not for love.
> —Rosalind in *As You Like It*

Some final don'ts and do's. Lend your speech vowel appeal, *don't:* strain from the throat, cut vowels short, channel them through your nose, or pull back your lips. *Do* give vowels easy, forward placement. Let them sound from released throat through relaxed mouth on the Good Breath. Lean on their length for sustained tone.

For basic distinctness in pronunciation, practice with these vowel wheels. Between the two of them, they contain all sixteen vowel sounds of American English.

Vowel Wheel I

This wheel consists of eight vowel sounds in comparative words. The first four spokes (1 through 4) exemplify the vowels /ē/ĭ/ā/ĕ/;

the next four spokes (5 through 8), the vowels /ă/ī/ä/ŭ/. Keep going around the wheel clockwise until you can enunciate all eight vowels clearly in the words.

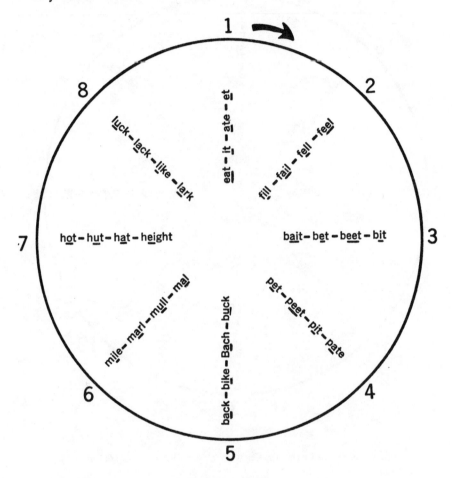

From *To Sing in English* by Dorothy Uris. Copyright © 1971 by Boosey & Hawkes, Inc. Used by permission.

Vowel Wheel II

This wheel consists of eight vowel sounds in comparative words. The first four spokes of the wheel (9 through 12) exemplify the vowels /ûr/o͞o/ū/o͝o/; the next four spokes (13 through 16), the vowels /ō/ô/oi/ou/. Keep going around the wheel clockwise until you can enunciate all eight lip-rounding vowels clearly in the words.

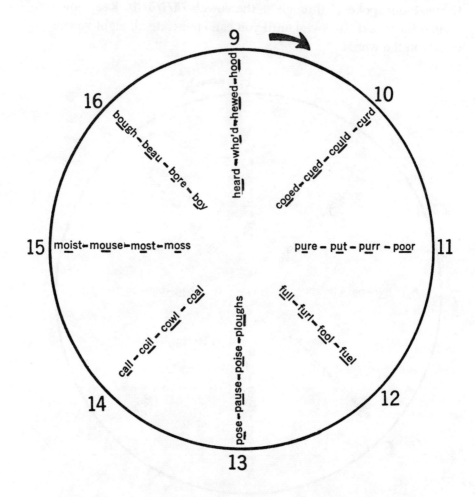

From *To Sing in English* by Dorothy Uris. Copyright © 1971 by Boosey & Hawkes, Inc. Used by permission.

Consonants

With a few martinis, consonants can practically disappear, "What's the idea?" becomes the heavy-tongued "Whassee-ieea?" And even without martinis, your tongue will grow flaccid, just like an arm or leg, from lack of use. The slip-slop habit of lopping consonants off, especially at the ends of words, weakens muscle and meaning.

What's inside? With pocket flashlight and mirror, have a good look around inside your mouth. Notice, behind your top teeth, the hard palate or domed roof of the mouth. At its forward edge, spot that important bump, the gum ridge. Back of the hard, you see the soft palate, which is a spongy mass. The uvula, a small pendulous lobe, hangs down from that. At the bottom lies the tongue, the only truly mobile member.

We'd have no /t/ or /d/ or /ch/ or /j/ without the quick touch of tongue tip to that gum ridge; no /l/ or /n/ without the sustained pressure of the tip on the same vital bump; no /k/, /g/, or /ng/ without the soft palate against which the back of the tongue operates. And if the lips couldn't come together, we'd have no sound of /p/, /b/, or /m/. We have twenty-five consonant sounds—nearly all athletic.

1. *The beauty prize.* Consonants bring character and vigor to all utterance. And some of them have beauty, regretfully often hidden, to match that of the vowels. First beauty prize goes to the three humming sounds, /m/, /n/, and /ng/, which give off the *right* nasal resonance. They fill head and throat with vibration, winding like a ribbon of resonance from word to word.

"The Highway*man* ca*me* ridi*ng*, ridi*ng*, ridi*ng*." Try lingering on the /m/, /n/, and /ng/ in your "Good *morning*," for breakfast-time morale some rainy Monday A.M.

2. *Lyrical /l/.* "I hear *l*ake water *l*apping with *l*ow sounds by the shore." Runner-up for the beauty prize is /l/, another favorite of poets. How many times do you hear "aw right" when things are *all right?* Learn to id*l*e a *little* on the mu*l*titude of /l/'s in a*ll* conversation.

For a more mellow /l/: press the tip of the tongue lightly, but firmly, against your gum ridge. The relaxed tongue does not touch at the sides; the back of the tongue must be low and free of tension.

3. *The buzzing sounds* /z/, /v/, /th/, /zh/, and their whispered counterparts /s/, /f/, /th/, /sh/. To let any of these sounds escape us robs our words of clarifying strength. Some lucid lines of poetry for practice:

Mu*s*ic, when soft *voices* die,
*V*ibrates in *the* memory;
—Shelley

Sweet is plea*s*ure
after pain.
—Dryden

_Th_rice be the _th_ings I _sh_all never attain
Envy, content and _suffic_ient _ch_ampagne.
    —"Songs of Perfect Propriety" by Barab

4. _Gliding consonants_ /r/, /w/, /y/. These have a dual nature: they move like consonants, but have vowellike qualities. Listen to them in:

Weep all _y_e little _r_ains; _w_ail, _w_ind, _w_ail.
                    —Folk song

5. _The lively percussives_ /d/, /b/, /g/, /j/ _and their whispered counterparts_ /t/, /p/, /k/, /ch/. Abundant in our language, these crisp sounds bring us their attractive pulsation. Work for the agility in tongue tip and lip essential to precise articulation of these stop-and-go consonants. Now try this excerpt from an Amy Lowell poem:

I wal_k_ _d_own the _pat_terne_d_ _g_ar_d_en _p_aths
In my _st_iff _b_ro_cad_e_d_ _g_own.

Some Prescriptions for Troublesome Consonants

1. _"Thing a thong of thikthpenth."_ No question, that's a _lisp_, an extreme one—the lingual-dental type with tongue seeking the teeth for /s/ and finding /th/. But perhaps you suffer from only a slight lisp (if _you_ don't, your friends do). Cute at three, but at thirty-three?

The fine muscular adjustments to a grown-up /s/ require patient practice. Please, no excuses about your teeth. While some malformations might encourage a lisp, tongue and mouth muscles can work around the dental problem to produce a clear /s/. Use these routines for any less-than-good /s/.

Remedies:

The /z/ _approach._ Since not everyone lisps both /s/ and /z/, first look to /z/. If your /z/ buzzes clearly, you're in good shape; /s/ is /z/ with the same execution minus voice.

Buzz and hiss. Imitate a bumblebee, then hiss the villain. _Buzzzzzzz—sssssssss._ Having removed voice from /z/, discover a correct /s/. To the point, some words:

zoo—sue	rise—rice
zeal—seal	buzz—bus
zone—sewn	his—hiss

The /t/ approach. Articulate t-t-t-t with precision on the gum ridge and keep at it. A strengthened tongue tip is vital for a good /s/. Graduate to words:

team—steam	tool—stool
tick—stick	tone—stone
take—steak	talk—stalk

Next, a verse:

> _St_ar light,
> _St_ar bright,
> Fir_st st_ar I've seen tonight . . .

Did your tongue bypass the teeth on /s/ and reach instead toward the /t/ position?

The /e/ approach. Whisper /ē/, holding the tongue high in the mouth. Seal off the air with sides of tongue against back teeth. *Focus the /s/* out of the mouth at dead center. Ready to sample the verse:

> How _s_weet the moonlight _s_leeps upon thi_s_ bank . . .
> Soft _s_tillne_ss_ and the night
> Become the touche_s_ of _s_weet harmony.
> Sit, Je_ss_ica.
> —Lorenzo in *The Merchant of Venice*

Some simple solid advice. A good /s/ is a short sound. A little sibilant goes a long way. Make it cleanly, and let it go.

2. Bye-bye, baby. Another carry-over from infantile speech is the lolling /l/ and /r/. Instead of /l/ we hear something resembling /y/ (I yove you) and instead of /r/, a /w/-ish sound (a wed, wed wose). Funny in that cartoon world of "wascally wabbits," but not in ours.

Remedy for babyish /l/. Discipline a lazy tongue. To sharpen tongue tip, chant: l̲a-l̲a-l̲a, l̲o-l̲o-l̲o, l̲ay-l̲ay-l̲ay, l̲ove-l̲ove-l̲ove.

Of course, articulate all /l/'s wherever found. No /l/'s are disposable except for those in words like *salmon, folk, talk.*

Remedy for ailing /r/. To drive home the essential difference between /r/ and /w/, use a mirror to observe that for /r/, lips hold still with the *tongue tip firm.* For /w/ lips move back for the next sound as tongue lies at bottom with the *tip passive.* Carry forward the correct action with:

reap—weep	rage—wage
red—wed	run—won

Try this daily drill to keep /r/'s resonant, up front, and out of the throat to avoid the gargled Amurrican /r/ sound:

no-no-no
toe-toe-toe
low-low-low
row-row-row

3. *The /ng/ click.* Easterners, especially, are plagued by this intrusive *guh* . . . sing*guh,* tongue-gon-rye. Important: /ng/ is not /n/ plus /g/ but a *third,* humming, sound, produced with tongue held quietly, tip down.

Remedy: With hands on ears, say *ring;* feel the hum as you hold the final /ng/ sound. This accurate sensation of /ng/ resonance should not be confused with the guttural quality of /g/. Hold on to the /ng/ hum. Compare:

hug—hung	wig—wing	hag—hang
rag—rang	brig—bring	rug—rung

Keep at this until transition is smooth from vowel to /ng/ hum. Go on to phrases: goi*ng* out, wro*ng* answer, ha*ng* up.

The Do and Don't List

—Articulate all the consonants most of the time (not just in special company).

—Develop the feel of vibration, hum, or voicelessness of tongue movements and the action of lips and teeth. Remember: *If you feel it, they hear it.*

—Watch overcorrection, please!

—Don't strain or mouthe; move the articulators only as necessary. Keep the jaw out of it. *The jaw is not an organ of articulation.*

—Don't merely tack the consonants on. Support them along with the vowels.

Now show off with this good exercise from a poet. Note that the poem contains twenty-one out of twenty-five English consonants. Which ones are missing? *

A Charm for Our Time

HIGHWAY TURNPIKE THRUWAY MALL

DIAL DIRECT LONG DISTANCE CALL

FREEZE-DRY HIGH-FI PAPERBACK

JET LAG NO SAG VENDING SNACK

MENTHOLATED SHAVING STICK

TAPE RECORDER CAMERA CLICK

SUPERSONIC LIFETIME SUB

DAYGLO DISCOUNT CREDIT CLUB

MOTEL KEYCHAIN ASTRODOME

INSTAMATIC LOTION FOAM

ZIPCODE BALLPOINT

—BURN BURGER BURN!—

NO DEPOSIT

NO RETURN

—Eve Merriam

* The missing consonants: /th/ (as in *the*); /y/ (*yes*); /wh/ (*when*); /zh/ (*beige*)

Essential English Linkage

So far we've been working with vowel and consonant sounds in isolation, abstracting these individual sound units from the mass of words. We divided to conquer; time now to assemble the pieces.

Think link. Bind consonants to vowels and to each other to syllables and words. Regard spaces between words as an optical illusion; it is where linking is most apt to break down. Learn to connect sounds across boundaries of words.

In union, strength. For our language to be communicative and persuasive, we must link words into *coherent groupings* and use pauses with purpose. Since the listener best discerns our meaning not in disjointed sounds and illogical breaks but in smooth sequences, women should learn to send their messages to the receiver in the manner most readily understood.

Your Voice in Good Health

We've been through the mechanics—from the sound of our voices to the sounds of the language. Before the next step of putting the sounds together into words and then the words into life and conversation, let us stop and consider how to take good care of the instrument that does the talking. What should we *do* and *not do?*

1. *Resist noise contagion.* As the decibel count rises, so do voices. Withstand the temptation to take the pitch of the crowd, or the clatter in restaurants; speak *under* the din, not over it. Noise pollution, so much with us, can cause hearing loss (statistics on the constant impact on young listeners of blaring rock music are startling).

2. *Don't take it out on your vocal cords.* Anger and frustration probably injure more voices than the common cold. So take it easy—harassed teacher, scolding mother, tensed-up job-holder. Emotion can grab you literally by the throat.

3. *Don't keep reaching for the gargle.* Doctors prescribe gargling for infections, not for bathroom exercising. Give nature's bodily fluids a chance to lubricate the mucous membrances of nasal and throat passages. The same goes for our addiction to lozenges; constantly coating the area with a sweetish film interferes with the natural action of cilia (hairlike projections) lining the membranes.

4. *Watch extreme temperatures of food and drink.* Our passion for the freezing flow of iced beverages down our gullets can have a distressful effect on sensitive tissues. And ditto for burning-hot liquids.

5. *Well, what about smoking?* If you have a steady tickling sensation and a cough, figure it out for yourself (or ask the Surgeon General). Coming from a woman, the inveterate smoker's croupy sound falls even more harshly upon the ear.

6. *What about alcohol?* If a drink brings tears to your eyes, it will also lacerate your throat. Certainly the combination of ice plus alcohol plus chain-smoking adds up to far from dulcet tones the morning after.

7. *Avoid constant clearing of the throat.* The more you clear, the more you feel you have to—a vicious cycle, triggered by nervous habit. The action involved grinds on your vocal cords. Cough, instead, bringing lower supportive muscles into play, or simply swallow.

8. *Guard your voice when you're tired, run-down, or ill.* Old speaking habits will attempt to creep back in, after all the gains you've made. If you have a sore throat, resist the tendency to speak back where the ache is (like scratching a sore instead of allowing it to heal). Try your humming exercise in a soft key; put tip of tongue between teeth as you hum *up front*—a soothing therapy. This will also help to ease a postnasal drip, a common complaint in our air-polluted cities.

Vocal Age

What are vocal wrinkles? Few women think they show, much less know they exist. The most obvious earmark of age is the quaver, a kind of cliché tremolo from cracks in the vocal line. In reality, however, many older women retain youthful, toneful vitality; on the phone, we can't guess their age; they could be forty-seven or seventy-four. The vocal mechanism is notably long-lived *if* we take care of it. (It beats eyes and ears in endurance and resilience.)

What causes the voice to age? All the faults we've discussed will hasten the onset of vocal wrinkles: choppy breathing, the habit of speaking in short snatches, and an uncertain pitch range. Another symptom is the guttural rumble of women who seem to sit back with a middle-age spread on their vocal cords. Tones, like the sitters, grow flabby. Yet it's never too late.

Combatting the decline of muscle tones calls for a corrective regime with no days off: reinstating the Good Breath, sustaining a long /ooo/ for twenty-five seconds, repeated ten times, and choosing from an assortment of other first aids (p. 28). Also important is practice speaking using longer phrases, without pushing the breath, trying not to break the tonal line and giving the key words full value.

For Everywoman regardless of age. Read aloud, checking with the mirror for pouting, puckering, yapping, and a set mouth—all these intensify lines around the mouth; the cheek area should remain quiet and composed.

The years can bring ripened, more resonant tones along with a higher content of rapport. A commitment to life, to work, to leisure, keeps women vital. And to this, add voices.

5

Word Wealth

A woman's vocabulary can provide her with a foolproof asset anywhere. With a ready-to-use stock of good words, any missing degrees after her name would go unnoticed in her conversation or in holding forth from a dais. The power of spoken language goes much deeper than external verbal trappings. As a priceless medium of exchange, expressive words enrich both talker and hearer.

Nowhere does conformity show up more than in our monotony of word usage. At bottom lurks the fear of sounding different. And thus, instead of keeping up with the Smiths, we all tend to stay down together.

Much of the airborne chatter and printed matter prepared for our rapid consumption is forgettable. Actually we *do* counterbalance the trite wordmongering with a literate press and stimulating magazines, slick and unglossed alike. And while critics wail over the low standards of radio and especially TV, the discriminating "singles" and "marrieds" (some new word coinage) can tune in to excellent talk most evenings and practically all of Sunday.

Time for spring cleaning. In the wake of women's greater involvement in "what's happening" (colloq.), life-styles have altered and so has language. Old words have been discarded or refurbished; newer or fresher ones "tell it like [*as!*] it is." Even the marriage ceremony tradition has been breached by new brides who choose to create their own more personal rites with language to match.

Every women knows that her reading vocabulary is more extensive than the one she airs in speaking. (Women are the nation's leading book buyers.) We all recognize and understand thousands of words in printed context, along with those heard in lectures and in TV and radio discussions. Instead of *"ubiquitous* Gloria," we'd probably say, "Gloria is everywhere at once." Or for *obfuscate,* which almost never seems to get off the page, wouldn't we prefer *confuse* or *obscure?*

The language admired in silence on printed pages is a source to tap for speaking. Of course, many words will remain *eye* words and rarely spoken, even by the most scholarly types (gamogenesis, coadjutor, inextirpable). Unless words have *use value* for you, do not choose the unusual or decorative ones for their eye appeal alone. Remember, you have to live with them.

More *eye* words must become *ear* words to furnish us with the speech tools essential in our complex communicating lives. Women are "into" (slang) politics, law, psychology, ecology, medicine, social services—and in all these pursuits they need words, and more words.

When reading, the only way to bring the little black symbols to life is to take them off the page and give them voice. To assume reality in your mind and in your ear, words must be *said in context.* When you've used a word by association in this manner it's almost yours. To own the word outright, you'll have to perform it. If you try to do so unrehearsed, however, you may lose the courage to speak it at all, or run the risk of fluffing if you do.

Now reach for your Speech Diary, and follow this form. In this way you prepare for the moment of delivery, when you communicate with a listening ear. Let us assume you have chosen the words *anomalous* and *perfunctory:*

New Word (*say* it)	Word in Context (*read* sentence aloud)	My Sentence (*speak* it)
anomalous	How *anomalous* was George Sand's masculine attire in 1834 during her tempestuous romance with Frederick Chopin.	Today there's nothing *anomalous* about women in trousers.
perfunctory	She gave me a *perfunctory* smile and again became immersed in the magazine.	It's a mistake to give the political caucus only your *perfunctory* attention.

If your chosen word does not reveal its meaning clearly in the written context, turn to the dictionary for help. You may have to dip into it several times until the meaning stays with you. If you're uncertain of the pronunciation, check with the dictionary's pronunciation key. After you've gathered a few entries, carry on with your cassette, and record words and sentences.

Take advantage of your practice with clear vowels and consonants. When you chit-chat you may become careless, but note how your voice and articulation improve when your intent becomes serious. Once you have *seen ... written ... spoken ... heard* the word, it is yours for the saying.

What's the Good Word?

Small packages. A large vocabulary does not mean a vocabulary of large words. Vigorous ones often come shorter. A sampling of some selected at random:

lad	imp	vex
nab	odd	tote
vie	ape	yen

Mouth-fillers. "Never use a dressy word if a simple one will do" is just the kind of advice that lazy minds can do without. We have some very choice three-, four-, and five-syllable whoppers:

flabbergasted	lugubrious	nincompoop
scalawag	lackadaisical	cantankerous
rambunctious	pandemonium	ignominious

Vivid verbiage. Large, self-conscious dictionary words can be a drag in any conversation. But do lift (colloq.) the many lively alternatives that you chance upon—those with strong *use* value. Add them to your stock, replacing the worn items. Why not try:

callow *for* immature	volatile *for* changeable
cajole *for* coax	fatuous *for* silly
desultory *for* aimless	rancor *for* bad feeling

Some relatively uncommon words:

buoyant	timorous	poignant
impeccable	querulous	succinct
erudite	intrepid	nuance

Bread-and-butter. Colloquial does not mean *lax.* Rather, the term describes the familiar and informal words that spark our talk. The absence of colloquialisms in conversation would lead to stilted phrasemaking and posturing. For women on the move, informality in word usage best expresses their fluid attitudes and working relationships.

Recognizing the utility of this live, contemporary speech, dictionary makers continue to include scores of words marked *colloq.* This informal language is constantly shifting; colloquial words make the grade to standard usage and, at the other extreme, slang words work up to *colloq.* Here is a mixed bag (colloq.):

brainwash	flop	pan out
buildup	flunk	pizzazz
cahoots	hassle	pro
chip in	in a jam	racket
comeuppance	jellyfish	rake off
corny	jinx	snitch
dirt	jitters	snoop
egg on	mad about	spunk
fizzle	moonlight	squelch
flabbergasted	kickback	tacky

Slanguage. Our pervasive youth culture has deeply influenced the adult community—from hair to jeans to slang. Seldom before have we embraced so much pungent and experimental word coinage. In the past, slang terms have emerged from underground to join the respectable society of words. With hindsight we can see that those meeting a genuine need had the best chance for survival. A handful that made it:

handout	debunk
highbrow	steamrolling
graft	shipshape

All these now qualify as *colloq.* But which of the following will one day be blessed by the heirs of Noah Webster? Or even remembered! Would you like to hazard a guess?

split	put down	square
good vibes	right on	with it
spaced out	pad	up tight
out of sight	cool	rip off
psyched out	heavy	cop out

Fresh and colorful slang words can be effective shortcuts in speaking and writing. *Put down,* a good example, may mean just what you want to say, taking the place of—*insult, deprecate, demean,* or *give short shrift to. Cop out* suggests self-serving reaction, irresponsibility, shirking one's duty, circumventing obligation or untrustworthiness, but *cop out* says it shorter and possibly sweeter.

Of course, a little goes a long way. But to frown on these terms and rule them out of circulation is nonsense when so many use so much so often. Such people-oriented parlance will prevail despite finger-wagging authorities. Time alone will tell (cliché).

Absence makes the heart grow fonder. Cliché comes from the French word *clicher* meaning "to stereotype, to cast from a mold." We have an incredibly long list of these ancient wheezes with built-in truth. They are not inexpressive, simply worn out to the point of little return. Women should avoid triteness which can no longer represent accurately what they need to say. Think of something *new* for:

those are the breaks	fresh as a daisy
the way the cookie crumbles	gild the lily
age before beauty	heart of gold
apple of one's eye	it goes without saying
beard the lion in his den	it stands to reason
blushing bride	pretty as a picture
bosom of the family	pure as the driven snow

cherchez la femme	make a clean breast of
fair sex	let one's hair down
feather in her cap	like a newborn babe

Too close for comfort. Do you know the difference in meaning between the words grouped together? Often the distinction is too vague:

| affectation | aggravate | wise |
| mannerism | intensify | expedient |

| excuse | laughable | rare |
| apology | ludicrous | scarce |

| despise | zealot | regret |
| disdain | bigot | remorse |

Confusion is rife. Listed below are sets of words often confused. Can you clear up the difference?

| stationary | effect | ability |
| stationery | affect | capacity |

| eminent | principle | complement |
| imminent | principal | compliment |

| definite | council | anxious |
| definitive | counsel | eager |

Wrong and right. Some chronically mispronounced words:

ath-uhletik	athletik (athletic)
champeen	champeeun (champion)
extra-ordinary	extrawdinary (extraordinary)
lenth	length (length)
strenth	strength (strength)

Note: Formerly, what were errors in some words are now listed as second and acceptable pronunciations. Which are these?

gynecologist	longevity
despicable	pronunciation
cache	tumult
culinary	vanilla
impotent	accidentally

Geographical variety. Different areas have their own favorite pronunciations. Just be sure your selection *is* included in some dictionary.

amateur	am-uh-tyoor, am-uh-ter, am-uh-choor, or am-uh-cher
adult	*a*dult or a*dult*
almond	amond or ahmond
amen	aymen or ahmen
either	eether or eyether
automobile	*au*tomobile, auto*mo*bile, or automo*bile*
forest	fawrist or fahrist
leisure	leezher or lezher
tomato	tuhmayto or tuhmahto

A short history of how women have come up in the world. If we want to go back far enough, we'll find that once when a girl had *charm* she would have been in danger of being beheaded for possessing magic powers. *Daughter* is derived from the word that meant the girl who milked the cows. *Homely,* once a flattering term, meant virtuous, and as for *lady,* she was just the member of the family who made the bread.

A hundred-year gestation gave birth to frankness:

> 1856—"She has canceled all her social engagements."
> 1880—"She is in an interesting condition."
> 1895—"She is in a delicate condition."
> 1910—"She is knitting little booties."
> 1920—"She is in a family way."
> 1935—"She is expecting."
> 1956—"She's pregnant."
>
> —Harry Golden, *For 2¢ Plain*

The Dispensables. Take the tired threesome of *marvelous, great,* and *divine.* You won't miss them once you've come up with:

superb	remarkable
rare	flawless
splendid	masterful
delightful	distinctive
	or just pleasant

And oh, that *nice!* How about:

kind	choice
agreeable	tasteful
charming	admirable
	or just fine

For the catch-all *okay*, substitute:

fine	decidedly
certainly	of course
surely	positively
	or just yes

Awfully can become awfully tiresome. For a change try:

considerably	unusually
exceedingly	extremely
	or just very

The dictionary fairly bursts with vituperation. For the slangy and weary *lousy* the choice is wide:

repugnant	hateful	scurvy
repulsive	nasty	vicious
putrid	pernicious	vile
despicable	foul	wretched
worthless	rascally	abominable
ruinous	malignant	
		Had enough?

Other dispensable items: *cute, mad, got.* How many alternatives can you find for them? *Got*'s got about fifty.

Linguistic melting pot. Many words, once taken bodily from virtually every other language on earth, are no longer even thought of as foreign. From any paperback thriller:

The *assassin* [derived from Persian], emboldened by *alcohol* [Arabic], stabbed the *tycoon* [Japanese] who was asleep in the *hammock* [American Indian] under a *canopy* [Egyptian] of *magnolia* [French] trees. He *grabbed* [German] the ten thousand *dollars* [Bohemian] and fled in a *jalopy* [Mexican].

English smorgasbord. Contemporary foreign words add color to speech, but sometimes they seem to strain for effect. Make sure to select the comprehensible ones that truly communicate. Can you guess to which countries we are indebted for these?

bravado	kindergarten	dashiki
shampoo	nirvana	kitsch
kibitzer	crescendo	schmaltz
taboo	safari	ciao
discotheque	mensch	kaffeeklatsch
bonanza	incommunicado	avant-garde

Apparently, words constantly cross the Atlantic in *both* directions, often to the chagrin of Old World academicians. Recently, from a French newspaper: "Jean Dupont, un businessman très up-to-date, a donné une surprise-party dans son bungalow ce dernier weekend."

Some Short Words about Grammar.

Is it I or is it me? . . . or him or he, or will or shall? Don't be a stickler when it comes to precision grammar. But, of course, "Annie don't live here no more" won't do.

Never end a sentence with a preposition? That's nothing to worry *about* (or about which to worry!). Anyone can cover the ground rules for good grammar. Writing with care and discipline gives us the leisure to study sentence structure and it can't help influencing our speech. Recommended for wobbly grammar—the proverbial best seller, that little book, *Elements of Style* by William Strunk, Jr., and E. B. White.

The root route. The root system for vocabulary building relies on detection. You learn to spot the key to word meanings by their segments—fore, center, and aft, technically, *prefix, root,* and *suffix.* Unquestionably the system works, but you have to work at it. Here's how:

reiterate—to say again
advocate—to speak out for a cause

prefix	*root*	*suffix*
re (again)	iter (second time)	ate (cause, make)
ad (to)	voc (call, speak)	ate (cause, make)

The copious *not* prefixes include: *un-, in-, im-, il-, ir-, non-,* and *anti-,* as in: *unable, insatiable, impossible, illicit, irresponsible, nondescript,* and *antisocial.* With all this negative wealth, why not not use *not?*

Replace:

> not honest *with* dishonest
> not like *with* dislike
> not aware *with* unaware
> > *and*
> did not pay attention to *with* ignored

Small nuisances. Unclutter your talk by avoiding: *different than*—try different *from,* or *unlike. Irregardless* should be *regardless;* however, *irrespective* is okay.

Like—please opt for *as* instead. Current top slang *(unlikables): like heavy, like you know man, like, yeah—like wow!*

Type—that *type* job won't last *(type of* or *kind of,* will)

-ly—refrain from pinning *-ly* to the wrong ends:

no	*yes*
overly	over
muchly	much
firstly	first

Indispensable Guidebooks—Essential Tools for Word Research

The dictionary habit, we are told, separates the learned from the lewd (an obsolete usage meaning unlettered). Noah Webster compiled the first American dictionary in 1828, which included 70,000 entries and soon became a self-help best seller. Webster's Third New International, a noble descendant, offers us 450,000 and a powerhouse of information.

Three types of American dictionary make an ideal package. The handy pocket editions of the larger works travel light and are bargains. The desk-size variety, most frequently thumbed, include Webster's New World, the American College Dictionary, and others. Webster's Third New International Dictionary (Unabridged), a lifetime investment, invites browsing, especially for uncommon words and for its fascinating display of verbal lore.

Some dictionaries represent careless compilations copied from other careless ones. Why refer to a less reliable source when top-notch versions are available everywhere?

Dictionary Exercise

You might use a magnifying lens so as not to overlook the small print in your dictionary. For example:

tim′bre (tim′ber, tam′ber: Fr. tan′br) n. [Fr.; OFr.; see TIMBREL]. 1. the characteristic quality of sound that distinguishes one voice or musical instrument from another of the same pitch and volume. 2. in *phonetics,* the degree of resonance of a voiced sound, especially of a vowel.

Thus *timbre* interestingly connotes the quality of voice uniquely our own, and, as such, contributes a fresh descriptive word to apply to individual voices.

Now the pronunciation. An important rule: first locate the diagonal line appearing usually after the syllable to be accented (tim′bre). *Timbre's* accents (the *built-in beat*) fall quite naturally. When you spot the key accented syllable of a longer word, you'll find that the parts within the word will fall readily into line, making the whole business of pronouncing it that much easier.

As for the pronounciations, *tim* has a choice of two (usually the dictionary puts the preferred one first). If necessary, consult the guide, generally found up front. You discover that the vowel in *tim* sounds like the one in *is* and *hit.*

As for *tam,* the /a/ turns out to be the same as in *fat* and *lap,* and the second syllable, *re,* similar to /er/ in ov*er* and und*er.* The abbreviation *n.,* as you know, means noun, the *Fr.*—from the French. *OFr.,* Old French, explains that our word is derived from the same root as *timbrel,* an ancient form of *tamborine.* This stimulating association helps to fasten *timbre* further.

Up until now *timbre* may have just been an *eye* word. Put it to use to make it an *ear* word:

> "Her voice had such an attractive *timbre* over the telephone, and when we met I found it suited her personality perfectly."

The word *thesaurus* comes from the Latin meaning treasure. Peter Mark Roget's nineteenth-century *Thesaurus* was revised by his son John, then by his grandson Samuel, and in scores of reprints which increased the original by some 50,000 entries.

As a felicitous and functional companion to a dictionary, the collection of synonyms and antonyms with index fills the gaps when right words just won't come and enriches vocabularies with alternatives.

Develop the dictionary habit—thesaurus, too, to express yourself fluently with fine old words or with shiny new ones. Your effectiveness as a speaker and thinking human being will be thereby enormously increased.

Finale (Italian). For women who are *word-poor,* or *word-worn* but *word-eager:*

—Gather an attractive and useful verbal wardrobe in which to clothe your thoughts. Keep shopping around for fresh items.

—Learn by association. To memorize something is not the way to remember it for long. Pin down what you want to remember with something you already know.

—Keep your Speech Diary and cassette handy to record words in writing and on tape.

—Speak good United States. In sum this means: clear enunciation of sounds, reputable pronunciation, useful vocabulary, *plus*—a big plus—good voice production.

As you pursue words, the romance as well as the reality will lead you ever on. You will find no end to this love affair with English.

6

The Company Words Keep

Now let's have a look at some current language with special and varied coloration: the jargon of jobs and professions, of sports, of psychological terms, political idiom, chic patter, "loaded" expressions, and the creative usages springing from the women's movement.

It is entirely human to want to belong linguistically. To become facile with up-to-the-minute words, you need only to spend a day with a newspaper and a week with a book. Faddish labels come and go, and are fun to pass around. Expressing American *life-styles* (one of *those* words), the language of and for the moment belongs to the people who speak it.

Culled from the current spate in circulation, here are some listings:

Learn the lingo. It is no longer cute (if it ever was) for a woman to say, "Oh, I just can't add." Instead she will hasten to a night course in economics; our statistics-happy American industry demands confident familiarity with the shoptalk of *capital investment, percentages, productivity,* and the like. If you yearn for a title on the door and a Bigelow on the floor, latch on to the jargon and flash the slide rule!

Aeronautics to Zoology. Technical terms range alphabetically in the dictionary with over fifty special subjects, covering the slew of verbalisms we call shoptalk:

affettuoso	ecotone	igneous
BINAC	F stop	jus civile
coping saw	gyropilot	kilovolt
dual controls	helix	liquid-level sensor

matrix	roentgenoscope	wimble
nitrometer	skiagraphy	xylem
odometer	trigger tube	ytterbium
palindrome	umber	zymosis
quaestor	venue	

Obviously essential in specialized areas, little of this vocabulary has relevance in a social setting. As members of the nouveau working class, women should resist showing off their proficient technical palaver. Better save talking shop for co-workers; don't count on your friends' tolerance—you may be boring them.

The bull's eye. Sport terms in their infinite variety are surprisingly intelligible to most men and to more and more women. How would you score with this matching word game? °

1.	baseball	a.	bed posts
2.	basketball	b.	corn
3.	bowling	c.	birdie
4.	fencing	d.	mudder
5.	football	e.	love
6.	golf	f.	touché
7.	ice hockey	g.	half-gainer
8.	racing	h.	face off
9.	skiing	i.	free throw
10.	diving	j.	two-bagger
11.	tennis	k.	relay
12.	track	l.	split end

Psychologically speaking. The "all-the-go" sensitivity sessions, encounters, retreats, and group gropings (mental and/or physical) for both sexes bear a made-in-U.S.A. label. This preoccupation of ours with matters psychological has loosed a flood of terms which originated in psychiatric conclaves and in mental hospitals. Professional categorizing has been watered down in amateur parlance to words passed around the breakfast table. One wonders if such dabbling in serious terminology should not be more self-censored.

° Answers: 1j, 2i, 3a, 4f, 5l, 6c, 7h, 8d, 9b, 10g, 11e, 12k.

A sampling:

compensation—practically any self-indulgence
repression—self-denial, noble or ignoble
regression—she loves bubble gum
You're not brought up any more, you're *conditioned*
adjustment—to a new apartment or maybe a winter vacation
fixation—any notion or emotion strongly held
transference—any emotional attachment
manic—odd behavior
schizo—even odder behavior
neurotic—his mother made him wear galoshes
psychotic—made him wear ear muffs besides and a shawl
introverted—if you enjoy solitude
extroverted—if you don't
compulsion—just one more candy bar

Some snobbisms. Since class—along with speech—distinctions are breaking down, the *Always (?)* and *Never (?)* columns describe mainly artificial differences between the upper and lower crust. If this fine-line listing makes clear the more honest term, so much the better. Some words may sound amusing or old-fashioned or affected. Let your good judgment, not class, lead you to the choices:

Always (?)	*Never (?)*
party	affair
dress	gown
dance	ball
rich	wealthy
house	home
underwear	lingerie
stockings	nylons
nightgown	nightie
people in	company
dinner	eat
laundry	wash
hairdresser	beauty parlor
movies	pictures

Always (?)	*Never (?)*
sofa	divan
refrigerator	ice box
lunch	luncheon
waiter	garçon
friend	girl friend
fiancé	intended
go to work	go to business
stop by	come over

Why not, instead of "powdering your nose," or "going to the little girls' room," just get up and say "excuse me" and head for the toilet?

Watch your language. "Sticks and stones may break my bones, but words will never hurt me." But they sure can smart a lot—especially with thoughtless stereotyping. Take the "typicals," for example—the *typical* secretary, housewife, school teacher, phys-ed major, Jewish mother, or little old lady in tennis shoes. What's a *typical* anything? This pigeonholing of "types" demeans the speaker along with those typed. Even the slightest slur on race, national origin, or religion bespeaks bigotry, conscious or not.

Oh, girl! A secretary or administrative assistant aged twenty-five and up will hear her employer say over the phone, "I'll have my *girl* get back to you." When applied to a grown woman, whether servant or telephone operator, *girl* is as offensive as calling a black man *boy*. It trivializes them all, reducing an adult to a position of inferiority.

Watch, too, those guilt-by-association labels: if you're an ardent "libber," you must be a *lesbian;* if you want to make love not war and your hair reaches below your waist, you must be a *hippie* (and *unwashed*); if you're a blonde, you're *dumb* (or have more fun?); if you wear hot pants and leather boots, you must be a prostitute (or an undercover policewoman) . . .

Bite your tongue. Some of the old and new tags hung on women: babe, baggage, ball and chain, ballbreaker, biddy, bird, broad, chick, chippy, dame, dingbat, doll, frail, frump, floozy, hussy, little woman, my old lady, old bag, plain Jane, sexpot, shrew, skirt, slut, sow, strumpet, tomater, wench.

We all could cultivate a more civilized sensitivity to the potential power for evil lurking in words. Guard against conditioned verbal reflexes; unlike Pavlov's salivating dogs, *we* can control our impulses.

Recycled words, almost as good as new. Reputable vocabulary, around a long time, has been buffed up to a new shine. Shuttling from the press to conversation, these voguish words seem to turn up everywhere at once.

A smattering:

Charisma: Charm, attraction, allure, dash, and pizzazz come all wrapped up in the *charisma* package. Without this "blessing" you can't get elected or find room at the top or meet Henry Kissinger.

Low profile: Low or high, it used to be the one you turned to the camera. Now if low enough, take it to mean a not quite invisible diplomatic position, somewhat like the ostrich's but sneakier.

Posture: This term has nothing to do with straightening your shoulders. Contemporary *posture* connotes an official *stance* (a first cousin) on some supposedly weighty policy. Obviously, it isn't just *anyone* who can have a posture!

Visceral and gut responses: A strong twosome having to do with emotional and intuitive reactions as opposed to the reactions from your head.

Machismo: A recent addition to the many nouns already in play to glorify the *he-man* (that's an oldie). This import from south of the border surpasses them all in virility and sexual prowess—with a dash of arrogance. The prototype of machismo would look like Mark Spitz, but act like Burt Reynolds mixed with a little Robert Redford.

A quick roundup includes also: *viable, dialogue, thrust, hangup, career-oriented, life-style, rhetoric, unisex, hassle, paradigm, parameter, clout, escalate.*

Overworked, the list runs the risk of becoming *old hat* (one that bit the dust). Some women love to pass these words around like fashionable signals of belonging, apparently hating to let go. When their time is up, better throw them out with that coat in the back of the closet.

The political scene also sheds expressions to linger who knows how long—law and order, inoperative, options, overview, protective reactions. From the Watergate scandals: *surveillance, kickback, plumbers, bugs, taps, point in time,* and others.

Nonsex nomenclature. The labels that depict the occupations of today's women at work have proved outdated and unserviceable. Why the *-ess* endings for unisex jobs: janitress, seamstress, sculptress, postmistress, authoress, directress? Why not bookkeeperess or doctoress, for that matter? Illogical and outdated, these vestigial appendages have to go.

The language itself has held women in a vise by lagging behind the reality of change. If you seek a job as a *foreman*, the title itself acts as a deterrent. Gifted in design, you spot a "draftsman wanted" ad, which you fail, of course, to answer. The trend has turned as does the worm—naming the occupation by the work performed and leaving sex out of it.

The classified sections of the newspapers have eliminated sex designations. All jobs are no longer listed *male* and *female*. The Census Bureau has followed by changing fifty-two job titles for its records, including:

> foreman—supervisor
> office boys—office helpers
> shoe repairmen—shoe repairers
> airline stewardesses—flight attendants
> clergymen—clergy
> advertising man—advertising agent
> middle man—agent, processor, packager, distributor
> deliveryman—deliverer
> the men in the field—representatives, agents, staff
> the girls in the office—secretaries, typists, clerks
> a one-man operation—a one-person operation
> a five-man staff—a five-member staff
> men in high places—high-ranking officials
> man-to-man—person-to-person, one-to-one
> the best man for the job—the best person . . .
> ear man, eye man—ear or eye doctor, specialist

Ms. has made it. The antiquated "Dear Madam" has finally lost out, with few tears shed over her demise. Though the controversy over the appellation *Ms.* still simmers, increasing numbers of business firms, institutions, and government offices have been adopting the form —and not because they've all turned feminist. It just makes more sense to use *Ms.*, a neutral term designating neither *Miss* nor *Mrs.* and as impersonal as *Mr. Ms.* shields the divorcees, takes the onus from the unmarried, and builds the independence of the married. Diehards notwithstanding, *Ms.* is here to stay.

"Suit the action to the word and the word to the action" (quoth the Bard). In a major effort to suit the words to the times, the women's movement has birthed new word forms; some at first sounded strange, but in a few short years have become legitimate and on their way to the dictionary:

activist	humankind
consciousness-raising	male chauvinist
chairperson	self-image
feminine mystique	sisterhood
feminist	spokesperson

We must continue to free the masculine-oriented "mother" tongue from the burden of discriminatory and obsolete language.

From Words to None. Nonverbal communication, known popularly as *body language,* has created quite a stir recently, and there has been a spate of books and articles on the subject. Women in particular have been fascinated to discover how as they walk or talk their unconscious gestures convey meaning apart from words. But even the experts have hesitated to spell out a precise vocabulary of body movement. Here are some of the educated guesses:

Do we:

lift one eyebrow for disbelief (or for amusement or perhaps surprise)?

rub our noses in puzzlement (or because they itch)?

shrug our shoulders for indifference (or for lack of knowledge)?

slap our foreheads for forgetfulness (or for sudden thought)?

clasp our arms to isolate or protect ourselves (or just because we're more comfortable that way)?

Are you on camera? Perhaps we're taking these patterns of body behavior too literally. Certainly one can benefit from awareness (not self-consciousness) of what attitudes and gestures could be saying when we speak. The published information stimulates, although much of it does seem pretty obvious. Any competent actress portraying nervousness or anxiety can choose from an all-too-human assortment of revealing mannerisms: foot-tapping, finger-drumming, lip-biting, ear lobe-twisting, hair-twirling, cuticle-picking, and nail-biting. Indulge in one or a combination of these and, despite your calm exterior, we'll be on to you!

It's only natural. True enough, the body at times gives the lie to the tongue—just as does the voice. The salesperson (late afternoon) leaning wearily on the counter tries to snap to as you approach, then her tired voice intones, "May I serve you, madam?" (Obviously the last thing she wants to do.)

Mostly gestures do work in accord with words. As we end a remark, the head will droop slightly, the eyelids lower (and the last word drops!). As we announce, "I'm going out," we're very likely to add a forward wave of the hand or head, or with "I went out," a backward one. Winding up the question "Are you going out?" our chin lifts with the voice, and so it goes.

Face to face. Have you ever considered that communicating with language alone is practically an impossibility? A roomful of people in conversation, standing or sitting stock-still, would resemble a scene in a mental institution.

It's fun in reverse, however, to try to tune out all words for a while (not an easy thing to do, either) and observe the rest of what goes on. Watch how someone reaches for a drink to have something to hold, or chain-smokes, or leans against the piano, or concentrates on the cheese dip. Note how some people park themselves near familiar faces and how others gravitate toward a stranger.

Admiring the man opposite, you take in the posed manner, face in control, the deep rumble of steady tone—and then catch sight of his leg jiggling against the coffee table. And the attractive woman he's talking with, who keeps running her hand across the back of her neck as if she were smoothing her hair—could she be thinking, "He gets in my hair" or "He's a pain in the neck"?

Ready, set, go. The charm schools used to make a great to-do about how to enter a room—head very high, shoulders way back, and bosom leading the way. Of course, few winding staircases remain down which to sweep with a rehearsed gliding gait—like the Miss America contestants on the boardwalk at Atlantic City. Forget the glide, but don't slump into a room and flop into the first down-cushioned armchair.

An erect bearing (shoulders *released*) lends control to the bearer and is always desirable. On the other hand, postural rigidity freezes mobility and marks a highly tense and ill-at-ease guest or host. When comfortable inside your skin, you will look it.

Eye to eye. The power of eye contact cannot be overrated. The tiny muscular movement involved creates an effect magnified a hundredfold. Staring is reserved for objects, not people, but if you fail to look at people when you're speaking or spoken to, then the omission can signal loss of contact, lack of sincerity, or even a refusal of friendship. And think of how the interpretation of shifty eyes can vary—from deception (cliché of thrillers) and feelings of guilt to profound shyness.

Irritating beyond words is the false intensity and eyelash-batting of the avid socializer. More eye clues: rubbing the eyes testifies like a yawn that you're fatigued, or just plain bored. Toying with eyeglasses by removing them and placing the tip of the earpiece in your mouth could signify stalling for what to say next.

Fashion plus. With adoption of slacks as a universal mode, women also adopted freer body movement. They walk with longer strides, and stand with feet apart, and their leg-crossing now includes the more masculine "figure four"—one leg horizontally positioned and the ankle near the opposite knee. If this image bothers you, imagine yourself in a tight corset and a long hobbling skirt, mincing down the street—and then *try* to get on a bus!

The overall less inhibited, more expansive gestures cannot be described or dismissed as male carbon copies. Women and their clothes have freely adapted to new freedom while their body and its language remains unalterably female.

Don't crowd me. A guiding factor in all body language is the country of origin, undoubtedly a considerable problem for diplomats. Outgoing Italians will touch and nudge, ego-conscious Germans have a stilted posture, and the reserved English tend to limit their gestures.

We maintain our distance, dislike being touched, hate to sit in a chair warmed by others, and resent lack of elbow room in elevators. A Frenchwoman talks and moves in French. An American woman handles her body in a distinctively American way, seeming to walk inside a personal bubble. How interesting that whenever we gesture or make a move, the "physical" dialogue we convey is within the American idiom.

Preoccupation with what the body may or may not be expressing at a given moment detracts from needed emphasis on *improved speaking*. Women want to be more verbal, not less, and to expand their use of lucid language and expressive voice. As we investigate the speech skills essential for successful interviews, group discussion, panels, and public speaking, body movement will be discussed when necessary to reinforce these skills.

Speech Melodies—And What They Tell

Every language has its own distinctive inflection pattern or melody—a musical term that belongs to speech as well as song—and American cultural cross currents have produced a large variety. Yet we can all discern an overall national cadence that is ours alone.

The most basic inflections consist of *two glides and a wave*:

down ↘, up ↗, or down-up ↘↗, and up-down ↗↘

For example:

Mother: "Are you going out?" (*Up-glide* for simple questions.)

Daughter: "I'm going for a walk." (*Down-glide* for simple statement.)

Mother: "A walk! At this hour?" (*Waves*, not so simple.)

Individual speech melodies, of course, transmit a good deal more than just our American intonation, conveying the *intent* rather than the *content* of our words.

Women are given to overuse of *rising* inflections, not unlike a plane in tentative flight that seeks but never quite finds a safe landing:

Q. What's your name? A. Jennifer Brown.

Q. Where do you live? A. Washington.

Remember, at the very least, to say your name always with a *down-glide*, as if really sure of it.

A woman clinging to unconscious, up-glided melodies produces unfortunate "vibes" in her listeners, who can only wonder if she should be taken seriously.

"I don't believe that—*I really don't.*" *(Does she?)*

"The movie was terrible—*wasn't it?*" (Well, *was* it?)

Her fuzzy intonations seem to side-step commitment, as if seeking confirmation. Is this childlike cadence tied perhaps to the vocal image of herself at fourteen?

Affirmation and decision call for a down inflection (not a big drop).

"I'll be there." "That settles that." "Yes." "No." When we really mean something, the voice should descend in a clear curve of confidence.

But repetitive, descending inflections fall heavily on the ear. The opposite extreme from the tentative statement is the "executive melody"—determinedly downward on every word, turning every question into a statement, if not a command. Intended to assert firmness, these often arouse resentment:

"Will you take a letter."

"Will you check with Mr. Winston."

"Can you make it tomorrow at four."

Women executives should take the cue and reject the put-down melody (mainly male) in their search for authority. Women in responsible positions should frame their instructions and questions as *requests*. A change of glide does the trick:

"Will you please take the package to the mailroom?"

(Not "mailroom!")

"Will you have the memo Xeroxed and distributed?"

(Not "distributed!")

Emotional stability or lack of it is reflected by our inflections. Any melody out of control betrays some personal disturbance: the melodic monotony of a lack of desire to communicate, or the ups and downs of pitch variability in some garrulous speakers.

A *well-balanced voice* with control over glides, whether up or down, imparts a sure sense of harmony in any setting. With sweeping curves of hyperinflection, the atmosphere heats up:

"What?" not "What?"   (Extremely irritated or upset.)

"Of course not." (Not "Of   course   not!") (Hyperemphatic.)

"Stop"   "Stop" "Stop"   (The last will attract a crowd.)

Better turn down the thermostat *and* the glides.

Put friend cassette to work and *listen* to recordings of your offhand chatting on the telephone or wherever you are, and catch those misleading melodies. Can you *hear* or *hum* a *tune?* Then do a job on your own off-tunes, the patterns that weaken a woman's image. Once you recognize the debilitating effect of continuous up-glides, you'll be able to *change* them.

When women's inflections sound more "polite" than men's, so much the better. Which one of these is yours?

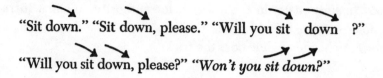

"Sit down." "Sit down, please." "Will you sit down ?"

"Will you sit down, please?" "*Won't you sit down?*"

If this last, "typically" considerate request is "female" intonation, let's have more of them.

Beware the *run-down melody*. Good American intonation means to sustain and *not* to drop energy on *down-glides* occurring at the ends of phrases. How often we lose a speaker's last word, along with the sense of a statement or question:

"How about meeting in the lobby of the Philharmonic at ten minutes to eight."

"*What time did you say?*"

Or:

"I'd like to place in nomination the name of Mary Tompkins."

Calls of "*Who?*" are heard.

The remedy for the voice that runs down? To the precarious last word, you can add an "and." Like this: "... ten minutes to eight *and*..." as if you were going right on. Or, "... the name of Mary Tompkins *and*..." Practice saying the phrase including the "and," but when you're speaking, merely thinking "and" will keep the last word from sagging.

If you work the mental "and's" routine on your cassette, you'll discover that the ends of your remarks remain intact—a distinct gain in speech melody and consideration for the listener.

Take a Break—A Poetry Break

For your instruction and pleasure, read aloud these poems, only three from the abundance of poetry now being written by American women. May Swenson, Erica Jong, and Eve Merriam, whose works vary in style and content, personify present-day voices that speak through a woman's perceptions.

The "now" content of these selections calls for speaking directly and unaffectedly—and of course distinctly. Note that the many run-on lines (the thought doesn't stop at the end of a line, but continues on) contribute speechlike rhythms. The first two sections of each poem are marked with slashes to indicate suggested stops for breathing. Finish the poems with your *own* markings.

Important: To inform and brighten your delivery, review the guidelines for reading aloud (pp. 37–41).

May Swenson was one of the pioneers of new techniques among American women poets. In the words of Pulitzer Prize-winning poet and critic Richard Howard, the effect of Swenson's work is "to charm, to enchant, to bind by spells . . ."

Maintain clear contrast between strong and weak word-types and syllables (the built-in beat, p. 59).

All That Time

/I saw two trees embracing.
/One leaned on the other
   as if to throw her down.
/But she was the upright one.
/Since their twin youth, maybe she
   had been pulling him toward her
   all that time

and finally almost uprooted him.
/He was the thin, dry, insecure one,
   the most wind-warped, you could see.
/And where their tops tangled
   it looked like he was crying
   on her shoulder.
/On the other hand, maybe he

had been trying to weaken her,
break her, or at least
make her bend
over backwards for him
just a little bit.
And all that time
she was standing up to him

the best she could.
She was the most stubborn,
the straightest one, that's a fact.
But he had been willing
to change himself—
even if it was for the worse—
all that time.

At the top they looked like one
tree, where they were embracing.
It was plain they'd be
always together.
Too late now to part.
When the wind blew, you could hear
them rubbing on each other.

Erica Jong, the young poet and novelist, says of herself, "Am a happily married feminist and very interested in the power of poetry to liberate women from old self-destructive patterns. And also to liberate men. Amen."

Note: If your tones seem trapped back in your throat, coax them forward with the pencil mike (p. 45) or the match trick (p. 49).

Alcestis on the Poetry Circuit

/The best slave
  does not need to be beaten.
/She beats herself.

/Not with a leather whip,
  or with sticks or twigs,
  not with a blackjack
  or a billyclub,
/but with a fine whip
  of her own tongue
  and the subtle beating
  of her mind
  against her mind.

For who can hate her half so well
as she hates herself?
And who can match the finesse
of her self-abuse?

Years of training
are required for this.
Twenty years
of subtle self-indulgence,
self-denial;
until the subject
thinks herself a queen
and yet a beggar—
both at the same time . . .
Though she is quick to learn
and admittedly clever,
her natural doubt of herself
should make her so weak
that she dabbles brilliantly
in half a dozen talents
and thus embellishes
but does not change
our life . . .

Eve Merriam's gifts run the gamut from myriad poems for children and adults to writing for stage and television. She had this to say about the collection in her book *Out Loud,* from which the poem "Rummage" is taken: "In all the poems, there are no invented sound effects. The words are all to be found in the dictionary. One of the joys of language is that there are so many ways to try to convey both musical tone and meaning."

This poem offers wonderful speech practice, so make the most of the vigorous variety of English sounds and shapes (*thirteen* different vowels, *twenty-three* different consonants). Watch out for the commas; stopping mechanically at the listed items is poor and boring delivery. Keep moving forward in the colorful flow of syllables and words, pausing only when necessary for a breath.

Rummage

/My mind is a catch-all
 of notions, ideas, sallys, a foray,
 scribble a jotting—

/like an attic trunk filled with junk:
 hodgepodge of rag-tag,
 worn-out boots, buttons,
/torn-pocketed vest, patchwork,
 dog-eared slack of postcards, crumpled Christmas wrapping
 twine tinsel tassels tangle snarl all knotted a snag of
/ski-pole bathing suit bent hanger dangling
 helter-skelter a clutter a scoop up of pell-mell
 beads beanbag hatbox wicker basket of higgeldy-piggeldy
/throwcloth float-cushion scatter-rug hammock hassock
 a jumble a stow
 sloven of stash ravel of stickpin grabbag—

Order! Order! straighten out this disarray,
 start filing, take inventory, build a shelf,
 classify, sort, throw away!

And I promise myself I will
 on the next rainy vacation day,
 but my mind doesn't mind me;
 saunters off in the rain
 and slinks back with more to pack:
 driftwood boat, lamp, table,
 stone for a doorstop, stone for a paperweight,
 and a gull's feather for tracing in sand
 notions, ideas, and—.

Negative practice, or the mimicry of your own errors, makes a
lively aid for dislodging stubborn habits. Here's how: while reading
aloud, try to parody the way you think you sound to others—perhaps
nasal, too high or too low pitched, too fast, mumbling, or monotonous. Obviously, here your cassette is a must. The deliberate dupli-

cation loosens inhibitions, sharpens self-hearing, and, most important, helps you identify the physical sensations that produce the faults in the first place.

You discover, for example, that if you have a nasal quality your tongue tenses and tends to stay high in the mouth. You then reverse this by relaxing the tongue with the tip down (especially on vowels). Resume reading with relaxed tongue, and your cassette will verify the nonnasal result.

Persevere with this before-and-after routine until it pays off in improvement. By coordinating the *new* sensations into your practice, you can achieve the *positive* effects of *negative* practice.

PART TWO

All
Speaking
Is
Public

7

Conversation, the Heart of Speaking

The *art* of conversation flourished decades ago when cultivated parlance was an essential social accomplishment in a woman. Well-born
young ladies learned the rules of polite discourse, how to play the
piano or harp, and to dabble in the arts. The novels of Jane Austen, the
Brontë sisters, Louisa May Alcott, Harriet Beecher Stowe, and many
others mirror the formal manners and ornate dialogue of their day.

From Jane Austen's *Pride and Prejudice,* let us read a witty exchange between Elizabeth and her suitor, Darcy (excerpted from
Volume Three, Chapter 18). Elizabeth wants Mr. Darcy to account
for his having fallen in love with her.

ELIZ. I can comprehend your going on charmingly, when
you had once made a beginning; but what could set you off in
the first place?

DARCY. I cannot fix on the hour, or the spot, or the look, or
the words, which laid the foundation ... I was in the middle
before I knew that I *had* begun.

ELIZ. My beauty you had early withstood, and as for my
manners—my behavior to *you* was at least always bordering on
the uncivil, and I never spoke to you without rather wishing to
give you pain than not. Now be sincere; did you admire me for
my impertinence?

DARCY. For the liveliness of your mind, I did.

ELIZ. You may as well call it impertinence at once ... The
fact is ... you were disgusted with the women who were
always speaking and looking, and thinking for *your* approba-

tion alone. I roused, and interested you, because I was so unlike *them* . . . What made you so shy of me, when you first called, and afterwards dined here? Why, especially, when you called, did you look as if you did not care about me?

DARCY. Because you were grave and silent, and gave me no encouragement.

ELIZ. But I was embarrassed.

DARCY. And so was I.

ELIZ. You might have talked to me more when you came to dinner.

DARCY. A man who had felt less, might . . . My real purpose was to see *you,* and to judge, if I could, whether I might ever hope to make you love me.

ELIZ. But I wonder how long you *would* have gone on, if you had been left to yourself. I wonder when you *would* have spoken, if I had not asked you!

Elizabeth and Darcy practiced the "art" of conversation and lived happily (we presume) ever after. What we have since lost in the elegant turn of a phrase, we have gained in frankness and in the reality of less privileged parlance. Fortunately, though, love still makes the world go round.

Though the "art" of conversation may have gone, we still manage to do a lot of effective talking. For "art" substitute "skill," which engenders study and the care and concern to communicate. While overworked, the term *communication* still expresses best of all the deepest civilized need—to reach one another with the spoken word.

The finished finishing school. Until quite recently, daughters of the upper classes were sent to charm schools to acquire ready-made formulas for elegant repartees and *tête-à-têtes* (whatever became of these?). Gone also are the elocution classes. In this country the word "elocution" long ago became the derisive term for artificial recitation complete with gestures. Unfortunately, the opposite extreme of naturalism, or the mumble school, is now very much "in."

Conversation, the "con" meaning "with." Verbiage merely as décor amuses us like that padded protuberance, the bygone bustle. The new elegance might be described as *the ability to say what one means with engaging voice and to share opinions with others in clear-cut, straightforward language.* Informality of approach matched with informal language lends itself especially to women's contemporary roles and the convivial, collective spirit from which good talk springs.

The Hidden Inhibitors (to good conversation)

1. *The hampering don'ts and do's.* Wishing to become a social asset, you seek textbook advice and discover how *not* to. Don't talk about yourself . . . Don't be aggressive . . . Don't talk about religion or politics . . . Don't gossip . . . Don't talk too much. In other words, don't talk! All these injunctions could tie the most facile tongue into knots.

And positive advice? Who could have all these on tap at once: Be cultured and tasteful . . . Be friendly . . . Be brief and sincere . . . Be animated and alert . . . Be restful, moderate, and modest. Concentrating on slogans, you're too busy to think of what to say.

2. *The one-way current.* TV features programs of other people talking—a spectator sport. These vicarious conversations prove that the programmers are on to what we're missing. But how much rubs off on the viewer? The dinner hour, ritual of relaxed chatter, may soon be extinct, as more of us chew away in semidarkness, TV dinners on laps.

Hopeful sign—a reversal trend in the recent resurgence of the lecture circuit. People are apparently growing tired of four-inch people on TV screens; they want eyeball-to-eyeball contact with life-sized speakers, to ask questions and try to determine more of the truth for themselves.

3. *Popularity contest.* Oh, to be liked at all costs! Straining after popularity keeps women's remarks small, safe, and dull. Shouldn't your freedom of speech begin at the talk level? This ever-smiling convention of social acceptability, ironically, does not guarantee popularity. Watch people gravitate toward the outspoken, offbeat speaker. Playing it safe conversationally, you mouthe what you don't believe or laugh at what's unfunny. How much healthier now and again to get hot under your pearls; any outburst that disturbs monotonous sound waves comes as a welcome relief.

4. *Is silence golden?* From covered-wagon folklore comes the

image of the hero and his spouse "yupping" their way through life. Around them has grown the myth that, because silent, they are necessarily deep—as if some inescapable contradiction exists between doing and speaking. There is none. The *woman of action* and the *woman of words* are one and the same.

5. *Time to desegregate.* The lowest ebb of a social evening has been reached when males and females in mute mutual agreement segregate to talk. This traditional separation of the sexes has seen some breakthroughs. The new mix has resulted in some blurring of roles with more women apt to talk about business and more men about food and cooking.

6. *Dispensable guests.* The floor hog who tells drawn-out pointless anecdotes. A statistical bore as well, she insists on "... was it Wednesday? No, it must have been Thursday."

Or the voice that nervously leaps into a momentary stillness with a favorite, safest-after-full-dinner topic—dieting. No help either is the eager beaver who intercepts others not so quick and glib as she, and that other social drag who hops from chit to chat shifting the subject just when the going is good. Equally dispensable count the show-me character who comes back smugly with "Me, I don't talk, I let the other girls talk ... I just listen."

7. *Repeal these prohibitions.* You must have heard that gossip (like sin) is something we are all against. But people are fun, so where do you honestly draw the line? One woman's gossip may be another's frankness: your anecdote, someone else's tattletale. Or *don't talk personalities?* How contradictory, and enough to make anybody feel guilty.

Air your prejudices but don't get the reputation as the woman who "can't stand" things. It matters little that you "can't stand peonies," and least of all to the peony.

How about "Don't be personal," another tongue-tying taboo? *Do* speak personally, for that makes you interesting. Sixteen or sixty-one, we are unique chemical compounds reacting to our one-of-a-kind backgrounds.

8. *Talking that never takes off.* We must also deal with our *self*-prohibitions, those personal lags that frustrate the urge that will not down—to speak with people and break the silence that isolates.

How does one find the confidence? How do women, usually silent when husbands or others speak, find the ways for their unaccustomed voices to respond? In an uptrend atmosphere of give-and-take, many who tended to be timid or withdrawn, or who overcompensated with forced friendliness, have begun to speak up with frankness and informed attitudes.

We must, of course, be wary of too-easy answers. We do know, however, that fluency develops with experience, that positive results can best be achieved by *doing*. The answers lie in *new* speaking skills to replace the *old* lacks and lags that inhibit self-expression.

It Takes Two to Make Communication

Person-to-person/person-to-people. Talk *with* people (not *at* or even *to*) underlies all speaking whether we're conversing one to one over lunch, participating in a panel discussion, conducting an office conference, or addressing a meeting—a small PTA gathering or a large political rally.

Good conversation, though generally considered just a spontaneous speech activity, actually depends on background, experience, and, above all, acquired skills. Particularly today, women require such conversational skills to smooth their path to successful speaking. For what they learn conversing in living rooms, they can carry along to the more demanding situations—in the boardroom, on the judicial bench, behind a lectern, on a dais, and before the U.N. General Assembly.

Listening

Learn to listen and listen to learn. Place high on the list of essential skills the ability to be a good listener. Speaking and listening are two sides of the same coin of our spoken exchange—50 per cent of the waking hours go into using one's ears.

We hang on to every word in any speaker-listener situation when we feel personally involved. For instance, at the yearly check-up, the gynecologist reads test results to inevitably avid ears.

Active listening divides into three interrelated actions—*hearing, attending, responding.* First your ear records mechanically the sounds of words. So far, no conscious contribution from you, but at this point too many of us just sign off. Due to the gap in the rate of speed between thought and speech, our minds can run ahead and off the path very easily. Estimates place thinking at 400 to 600 words per minute and average speaking at only about 150 words per minute.

Therefore, follow *hearing* by *attending;* that's where *you* come in, meaning you pay attention, what you'd expect of someone else. But don't sign off here either, for now comes the creative step, *responding.* Pick up the cue and answer. No need to come back with a quick retort; just an aware look can make a good answer. Avoid, of course, the blank expression since such unreactive behavior will dampen the spirit of any conversation.

The old one-way street. If you start daydreaming when a lecture-circuit celeb hits you as dull, remember there are no uninteresting subjects, only uninterested persons—and snap to.

Reacting to something that rubs you the wrong way, do you begin at once to work on a retort? Hopping on your personal train of thought, you've stopped attending and intake as such falters. Or, easily turned off by a TV personality's clothes, mannerisms, or accent, you lose interest in what she or he is saying. That makes you the loser—you may have missed something memorable.

Two-way traffic. Attentiveness deepens the esthetic appreciation that comes to us on the waves of sound. Neither language nor music has existence except as we receive it. Careful listening will make you a better student in and out of class; critical listening, a more enlightened citizen, and sensitive listening, a more responsive and appreciative woman.

Dealing with Yourself

The "I-should-have-saids." When the last guest has departed, we begin to fantasize splendid, humorous, informed answers—we get in the last word, pull off a snappy comeback, and so on dreamily. Internal dialogue after the fact is a common indulgence, and while these cozy post mortems may relieve frustration, we all know they do little to improve the fluency of verbal harmony.

Try a self-quiz to counteract flights of fancy. In a wide-awake mood, deal strictly with yourself and frame the queries honestly. Accurately posed, questions contain within them the key to answers. Obviously, no one person could be bogged down by all these hassles;

they reflect in general the personal snags that thwart fruitful interchange with others.

—*Why was I embarrassed* when the discussion turned to love versus sex . . . or whether to permit a daughter's boy friend to spend the night? . . . or what we parents should do when a bottle of pep pills turns up in the laundry basket?

—*Why was I intimidated* at meeting the mayor's wife, an entirely approachable woman? . . . or the professor of astronomy, a subject out of my realm?

—*Why was I belligerent* during the argument on abortion reform? . . . or the Equal Rights Amendment?

—*Why was I negligent* in allowing my mother-in-law to be excluded from the conversation at the family dinner? . . . or in cutting off my ten-year-old's breakfast chatter about her friend's birthday party?

—*Why was I garrulous* in persisting long after the discussion on a woman for vice-president was already exhausted? . . . or after everyone described a favorite yoga asana I kept harping on mine, insisting on demonstrating a headstand?

—*Why was I gauche* in asking the actress the same old question about how she managed to remember all those lines? . . . or the big-wig executive how she likes working in a man's job?

—*Why was I self-centered* in going on about my skill as a snorkeler when no one in the room was interested in my underwater activity? . . . or in giving out with the pictures routine plus cute sayings of my eight grandchildren who live in Cupcake, California?

—*Why was I backward* when I couldn't get the conversation started with the early arrivals at my dinner party? . . . or when, as hostess, I allowed the after-dinner talk to wind down instead of leaping into the breach with some fresh item?

—*Why was I ill at ease* on and off at the Smiths'? Was it mechanics—did my voice, out of control, become strident, the pace too fast, and why, oh why, did I try to pronounce *pusillanimous* when I could have said *cowardly*?

Are you out of practice? Perhaps it's time for a vocal check-up:

To lower the register that got away, return to some corrective measures. See *Reading Aloud* (p. 37) and speak the poetry or some stimulating choice of your own. When warmed up and with a more resonant and released tone, interpolate in the delivery some everyday remarks. "How nice to see you again." (Back to poetry) "That's a lovely dress." "Oh, no, it doesn't look old in the slightest!" (Poetry) "Have you read Lillian Hellman's *Pentimento?*" In this fashion keep improvising on your own so that practice will spill over into life.

In the gabble hour at cocktails or in a theater lobby when your pitch starts to climb, stop. Breathe out gently. Take a new easeful breath and counting on *feedback,* reestablish that pleasant tone you achieved during practice.

If at the embassy reception your voice seems to betray your nervousness, your mouth feels dry, and your words resemble a static of disjointed hunks of phrases, hark back to the *smooth blending of linked phrases* you achieved in reading aloud the night before. Again, take that comforting little breath and be careful not to stop and go arbitrarily. Let your thoughts lead to a logical *pause* that you can hold for needed relaxation. You will find your voice takes on new confidence.

As for *pusillanimous,* what about checking with your dictionary if you expect to spring an unfamiliar word on your friends and colleagues?

Do You Have Topic Trouble?

Do you tend to keep nervously silent at a gathering, held back by the tongue-tying notion that only extraordinary events in your life are worth talking about—or the latest weighty or arty subjects? So you've never had quintuplets, nor tried skydiving, or dined with Richard Burton. *Relax*—you can still make conversation. Any topic will do —almost.

Of course, it's civilized to skip the recounting of plots of films that others haven't seen (skip them even if they have) and of books that you alone have thumbed. You can spare listeners details of your aches and pains or anecdotes about brilliant children and adorable pets. Why not turn off as well the overflow of solicitude with older people? And cut down on the gooing when the pajama-clad resident siblings have slipped down after bedtime into the living room.

Otherwise go to it, if (and a big "if") the topic really grabs your interest. No one wants to listen to anything that doesn't. Often the individual slant and personal observation will do more to perk up listening ears than the topic itself.

How small is small? Seriously wondering what small talk to engage in? Then you're probably concerned more about social ease than about subject matter. We have an endless variety of comfortable chatter to serve as handles, and anything (even the weather) will do as a starter—if you really mean to start. Think of small talk as a curtain raiser, not the whole act.

Talking big. Conversation, a friendly pastime, brings warmth in sharing opinions and stimulation in differing with one another. It also provides the opportunity to exercise good speech habits. A careless performance only fortifies those past patterns you have been working to overcome. It's risky to have Sunday and Monday speech—when you reach for your *Sunday best,* your *Monday poor* may well slip back in. Or, like a split-speech personality, do you save your good voice for serious topics and turn on the high breathy one for the lighter moments?

To cope with practically any conversation: read, read, read.

> Reading maketh a full woman, conference a ready
> woman, and writing an exact woman.
> —Francis Bacon (without apologies)

Glance at the table of contents of any news magazine and find an alphabetical listing of broad topics: *behavior, books, cinema, economy and business, environment, medicine, nation, people, press, religion, show business and TV, sports, theater, world.* Everyone has a stake in any or all of these areas, furnishing enough talk to keep a modern Scheherazade going for 2001 nights!

As food for talk you can depend on the daily newspaper, weekly magazines, and a plenitude of many-splendored books. To find out how to do almost anything, it seems a book will roll off the presses to tell you—*how to survive as a woman, suddenly single ... how to understand your dog ... how to run your house without letting it run you ...* and so on and on.

Become a clipper. Read the press, scissors at hand to cut out what strikes your fancy. Underline in color the significant sections, paste the clippings in a large scrapbook, and enter the hot items in your Speech Diary.

As a self-improver, you can convert some of the likely material to reading-aloud practice, helping also to implant the content in your mind. The living room becomes a lab where you can experiment with your larder of live information. Not just a time-filler, this active routine of reading and speaking will enliven all business, professional, and social relationships.

Talking—Two or More

What's your angle? Conversational groupings keep shifting like a TV camera. Let us follow the roving lens, picking up a *group shot* (a roomful of talkers), then traveling to a *four* or *three shot* within the group. Now we focus on a *two shot*, a pair immersed in discussion or merely in banter.

Were we to hear the voices—ideally, they'd have adjusted to the size of the camera angle—the tones would be audible but not loud even in the larger setting; the words unhurried and communicative. The ideal is a reachable goal; *what* you say is important when your *how* bears it out.

Two is company. As the dialogue grows more personal, the performers move closer and the camera follows suit with the most frequent of angles, a *tight two* (delightful term). Two by two we win a job, an argument, a friend, a lover, or a mate ("Why go out, why not just stay in and talk?").

Story of a luncheon friendship. When the two women meet, their glances do not wander; they regard each other person to person with seeing eyes. "How did the interview go?" "I can't be sure." They talk awhile, then comes the point-blank question, "What happened after you showed him your résumé? I want details." She gets them. The two cooperating gladly (this is no one-sided counseling session) share the experience, which benefits them both.

In mixed company. Good talk is like a spirited game of tennis with the ball volleyed from one player to another. And no accomplished player, man or woman, would think of holding on to the ball too long. Topics range widely and bespeak changing attitudes.

> Women bone up on The Game (football)
> Bachelor fathers adopt more children
> John Wayne no longer the model of masculinity
> Redefining relationships
> Women marry men not names

Woman talk, a term in poor repute nowadays, has come down to mean a chatter-mix of cooking, shopping, and children—spiced with gossip. But women certainly do, and should, feel free to talk about what concerns them on matinee day or working day.

Conversing together openly with few taboos brings mutual release; knotty matters straighten out among groups of friends who really listen and try earnestly to relate a single problem to their general experience. Egocentric attitudes have given ground to greater trust and respect for one another along with pride in today's achievements by women.

Laughing Matter

> Humor . . . is rarely malicious; . . . but laughs its
> way into the heart. . . . Unlike the poisoned barb of
> satire and the killing point of wit, humor
> is healing . . . recreative and rejuvenating.
> —Louis Untermeyer

Women rarely think of themselves as raconteurs, the art of telling the humorous story having been pursued traditionally by men. As with other conversational skills, practice can bring confidence and competence in the relating of amusing anecdotes or the shorter punch-line variety. Mothers who enjoy reading or recounting stories to children have been rehearsing right along.

If you set yourself the goal of acquiring this pleasant social asset, you will need to do some research and to learn some ground rules. Begin by collecting the raw materials—books of light humor, magazines, newspaper items from the too-often outlandish political scene to those human-interest fillers tucked away in inside pages. Creating your own stockpile will forestall someone's ego-quenching complaint: "Not the one about the absentminded professor!"

Some Pitfalls:

1. Don't tell a story for the first time to an audience, even of one (well, maybe to your best friend). Practice aloud using your cassette, which by now has become a fruitful and comforting routine. Once you've gained security at home, delivery before a group will appear (on the surface at least) quite relaxed and smooth.

2. Keep your material brief and stripped of all extraneous detail. The skillful build-up can rivet attention, but better wait until you're more experienced.

3. Don't tell a story you can't finish. "I can't remember the tag, but it went something like this . . ." will generally write finis to your humorous effort of the evening.

4. Watch your advance sales pitch about the "terrific" one you've just heard and are about to repeat. This personal boost will turn every listener into a critic.

5. Take care not to give away the punch line at the start, as do many inept yarn-spinners. "Did you hear the one about the elephant's footprints in the aspic?"

6. Make it a rule to bypass dialect stories even if you're great at imitation. You can never tell—some susceptible people with a cool exterior may take offense. The response to this genre of questionable humor is rarely worth the danger of affronting anyone.

7. Don't attempt off-color jokes unless you can carry them off with aplomb. In these days of greater freedom in mixed company, the laugh-provoking subject of sex enjoys wider circulation. If you join in, make sure that your contribution reveals more wit than smut.

8. Very few of us can get away with laughing at our own jokes. Sometimes laughter will set off a contagion of chuckles—but it's risky.

9. Especially for listeners: after someone's gem of the evening you can skip the anti-climax of stating loud and clear, "When I heard that story, it took place in Africa not Australia, and it was a giraffe, not an anteater!"

You're on next. With a little encouragement, your innate acting ability will come to the fore to enhance your narration. Women have a natural flair for coloring their voices to express the emotions of characters they depict in storytelling—anger, shock, elation, joy. So let go and dramatize. Sometimes just the comedian's deadpan manner can be effective, especially with a clever story line or twist.

What's the right moment to spring your anecdote? Coming in suddenly from left field can be awkward. The best approach is to take your cue from the conversation and try to make your tale relevant to the remarks at hand.

Quick quips. The short joke is an embellished punch line, pared down for efficiency. It calls for simplicity, directness, and a straight face. You learn correct timing by doing. If you search for anecdotes about women to recount, you'll find the selection disappointing and disheartening. Most often the female turns out to be the butt of jokes that sound dated and unfunny ("that was no lady, that was my wife"). Here are typical put-downs:

"Papa," asked Junior, looking up from his schoolbooks, "what is a monologue?" "A monologue, my son," answered father, "is a conversation between a man and his wife."

"Do you believe in clubs for women?" a friend asked W. C. Fields. "Yes," replied Fields, "if every other form of persuasion fails."

Now try your skill on a few short ones worth the telling.

The other day my husband backed out of an unfamiliar parking lot and hit a tree. I behaved very well, sat quietly, and didn't say a word. He turned to me and said, "For heaven's sake, can't you look where I'm going?"

The old stock question came up again—"If you were to be marooned on a desert island with a man for the rest of your life, what man would you prefer?" Came the woman's reply, "The world's finest obstetrician."

Your Dial Tone

Over a hundred million daily telephone calls keep American wires humming—mainly, it appears, with women's voices (including those of fifty thousand telephone operators). Certainly all this verbal output deserves more attention than its customary offhand treatment.

We all marvel at the way a fine actress performs a telephone scene—with no one, of course, at the opposite end, she simulates such true rapport that you can practically *see* the other party. We can translate the essence of this technique into any telephone conversation. Mostly people sound as if they were talking to a dead instrument instead of a live listener. Like the actress, we should acquire the voice quality that reaches out to the real person *we* have at the other end.

When you pick up the phone, adjust to a person-to-person attitude and keep the caller in your mind's eye until time to hang up. Gestures add warmth to words even over the phone: your shoulders may shrug, head nod or shake, eyes respond, free hand move, and your occasional smile penetrate the wires. Let go of any tension by leaning back in the chair, holding the instrument lightly in your hand (a tight grasp will show up in tight talk). For tired, inert voices, tone up with an alert posture, a straight back, feet firmly on the floor.

Telephone tips. Some women with antennas for ears can spot trouble right off. "What's the matter . . . anything wrong?" The "ESP question" startles you. Of course, your tones needn't drip with honey all the time—be naturally responsive to the moment.

Point zero in telephone rapport is undoubtedly reached when the listener at one end holds the receiver at arm's length while the voice on the other end goes on and on . . . what a nightmare to imagine it might be yours.

Become a habitual note taker. Telephoning with pencil in hand encourages fluency when you need it most and prevents details from slipping your mind. For important calls you'll want to write some apt phrases or questions ahead of time, preventing afterthoughts.

Mind your telephone manners. Avoid: making the listener your captive (does she or he have time for personal chatter?); calling during dinner time (or breakfast, for that matter); keeping answerers in suspense (say who you are); chitchatting during a professional call (get to the point); hanging up with a bang.

Say goodbye as if you were extending your hand at the front door. An abrupt finish is like slamming a door in someone's face. Replace the receiver with a slight pause after your last word. Of course, with an objectionable phone call, just hang up.

Speech mechanics over the wire. Watch the excitement and tension that causes tones to rise; a lower pitch carries more pleasantly, so learn to speak in the lower half of your range. Practice until you can sense just how much volume you need; hold the mouthpiece at a distance to accommodate your carrying power—an inch to four inches away. Too loud, you come across impatiently or angry: too soft, you muffle your words—with either extreme, you strain the listener.

Speak distinctly; you don't have to say *feye-uv* (five) as the operator has been taught to do, but try to eliminate careless pronunciation, running words together or lopping off sounds at the ends. The appropriate pace for comfortable listening is generally somewhat slower than face to face.

That accessible little instrument affords a ready-made medium for your speech practice. Free from intimidating eyes, you can experiment with varied effects of voice production and try on some new language for size.

Family Talk

It would take another book (or books) to do justice to the importance of family communication, especially in view of today's changing household scene: the two-career set-up, single parenthood, divorced fathers with custody of children, and, most significant, the greater husband-wife sharing of chores and the time spent with their offspring.

While concentrating chiefly on woman's personal voice and speech and essential public skills, we can't overlook her still starring role in the home. Family speechways, the problems and pleasures, also some guidelines for futher investigation of a too little understood subject follow (see bibliography).

Parents tend to overindulge in an exclusive brand of adult-world talk that shuts out children. Let the children in. Three-way conversations (or four- or five-) create an atmosphere conducive to speech growth. True, the problems of family communication go deeper than mere talk, but a warm give-and-take climate can ease tensions, unravel problems, and e courage *unhurried conversation, pleasant voices,* and *a lively shared interest in words.* A respect for these tools will condition the homegrown, positive habits that show up later in alert and unhampered speaking voices.

Denying children entry into our world tends to prolong their ignorance and dependence. Perhaps it's time to make room also for the "liberated" child. Too little exposure to talk in the home means too little stimulation for her/him. In democratic family living, time for discussion and agreeable disagreement provides safety valves for young egos to let off steam (rules for discussion [p. 142] apply as well to the home).

To understand children in realistic terms, we need to sort out some of the notions that blur our communication with them:

—"Let the child be a child." (Protect the tender tots at all costs from the big, bad world.)

—"The best time of your life." (Who says childhood is happy and carefree? Certainly not the youngsters, who can't wait to grow up.)

—"Ah, innocence!" (This admired, vacuous quality is another fiction; children are serious, and eager to learn.)

—"Children *need* love." (In the first year or so of life, the cuddling and coddling are clearly essential; too soon after, the smothering gives only adults satisfaction.)

—"Children are *so* cute." (Our "cutesy complex" teaches children to exploit the trait; what kind of woman do these mincing steps and whiny tones produce?) Let us be done with the habit of marking children with a *cute* label. Let us instead respect their innate excitement, "up" attitudes, curiosity, energy—all their human attributes.

Some Guidelines for the Home

1. *Baby talk, the right kind and the wrong.* Communication between mother and child begins with touch and tone. Baby's babbling heralds an advanced stage; a dialogue of nonsense syllables ensues—reciprocal baby talk in an alphabet of love. A prologue to word-making, this essential game should be played consistently by mother or anyone substituting for her.

2. *Readiness, not earliness.* "Say hello to Grandma." "Come on, now, say goodbye to Aunt Tillie!" *Say, say, say.* Babies simply must not be pressured into talking *too soon.* But once she/he has achieved some word mastery, turn off the baby talk *(yours).* Refrain from "choo-choo" when the child can pronounce "train."

3. *A horrible example.* "I *thaw* a *wabbit,* Mommy!" (Laughter at this "adorable" lisped effort.) Then Mommy or Daddy imitates cutely, "Oh, *ittu* girl, I *yove* you!" Pretty risky behavior, since twenty years later, *ittu* girl (boys, too) might still be saying *yove* and *wabbit.*

4. *We are all models, especially mother (or her surrogate).* A child accumulates more than words: she/he stores away the accompaniment of *inflection* and *tone,* the language of the emotions. Along with *what, how* you speak reflects the pitch, quality, and intensity of voices in the home. Also contagious are some undesirable features: a sibling's lisp, a grandmother's quaver, a father's hesitating speech.

Though it may seem superhuman at times, try to speak amiably and lucidly and go easy on the tempo. Think of that little mind trying to grasp meaning from a flood of chatter.

Speech is a tool, not a toy. When moppets parrot brand-new, long words, restrain yourself from showing off their precocious vocabulary.

5. *Teach by indirection. Wrong:* "Don't say 'itter,' darling, say 'sister.' " *Right:* Insert the correct word casually: "Your sister is in school." Never hit head on with a correction; always make it oblique and smooth.

Identify words with life and reality, the labels with objects, the word with experience. Create fun speech practice: a homemade speech book, talking games, cassette tapes, records, and reading aloud (so good for *you*). Children seem never to tire of listening.

6. *Stumbling isn't stuttering.* Don't impose the family tempo; forced to get a word out fast, the child may not get it out at all. Speech wobbles should cause no alarm (especially when the young ones are fatigued or overstimulated); accept them without hint of anxiety—*none*, lest the child catch it. Children can sense alarm with supersonic perception; and in the name of sanity, *never* label stumbling "stuttering"!

7. *Take the heat off Mother.* Other influences beyond her control contribute to speech problems. The family, the first social entity a child experiences, mirrors the tensions of society as a whole.

However, when trouble persists at the age of seven or eight, seek help by consulting a private or school therapist, or apply at a hospital speech clinic.

8. *Really tune in.* Listen actively to childhood chatter with an ear for hidden messages; include also the nonverbal variety transmitted by tone, expression, and gesture. Watch your own body language: face your youngster, pause for a moment, take time out to talk. Express your own feelings to encourage her/him to do the same. Always, your voice modulation is a source of strength.

No formal stage is necessary for that irrepressible urge toward self-expression. Right at home children infuse the most mundane settings and objects with the magic of imagination. Make the most of their desire to perform *as if* on TV, radio, in films and theater—all of these make fine speech projects.

9. *And as for TV* ... Parents must continue to put pressure on government agencies and networks to cut down on the violence and the commercials that support it. Also important is monitoring children's programs and rationing the viewing time. By all means, let the whole family imitate and laugh at the voice stereotypes—the drawling, nasal, guttural characters—and without making it too obvious, invite the children to join in watching some exciting, well-spoken adult programs.

Some Guidelines for School

1. *Enter teacher.* Lucky are the children who find a teacher who communicates the excitement of learning in words that make vivid pictures and with tones that convey security and control. Unfortu-

nately, too few educators make such good speech models. We must share the blame in not pressing for required speech education for students at all age levels. No, we can't just "leave it to teacher."

2. *Rah! Rah! Rah!* Cheering and yelling for the team can often ruin maturing voices, especially during the adolescent voice change. A way to preserve the enthusiasm and spare the vocal cords: show these frenetic fans *how* to put their abdominal muscles to work in support of their vocal outpour (see p. 28).

3. *Combat sex stereotyping in early childhood.* Forestall especially those inhibiting speech mannerisms (weak, regressive, high-pitched) that women find so resistant to change later on. A positive procedure: encourage girls in more outgoing and broader-based play. Both sexes should sew, cook, do woodwork, and play ball—whenever feasible, together. Let them understand that for each, many options are open.

Select the excellent nonsexist books now on the market (see bibliography). Toys are the *result* of sex roles, not the cause. Rule out the militaristic items; otherwise boys and girls should freely exchange their playthings.

And this too shall pass: males will not have all the adventures, and even Barbie will have more to do than just change her clothes.

Understanding children better, we can better reach their understanding of us. Little ears sop up like sponges our honest and accurate words. Good speech, like good deeds, begins at home.

8

The Interview: Conversation
with a Purpose

Our most frequent and fundamental speaking activity, the two-by-two conversations, embrace as well the many forms of interviews that are so much a part of our communicating lives. The give-and-take quality of informal talk carries over to those face-to-face encounters where pleasantries are necessarily limited, and where we keep a *specific purpose* in mind.

Via interviews, we apply for a job, request a raise or promotion, gather information, resolve problems, or buy or sell something—all of which comes down to a need to *persuade* someone—at a given time and place, and usually with a time limit. The *business*, not the small talk, is the overriding objective, along with a hoped-for decision as the outcome.

Today's on-the-job woman has become aware that the essential skills required for successful interviews belong to all forms of successful speech: organizing ideas, analyzing the listener, and putting her best voice forward. She has been learning how to make good use of her innate flexibility to adapt these skills to the specific shape of the business (or businesslike) engagement at hand.

The Tools and How-to's

Industries usually conduct a two-level job interview: a screening by Personnel and then a quizzing by the department managers who have hire and fire power. The first gives you a foot-in-the-door opportunity to make an impression with Girl Scout answers, and it gives the interviewer a chance to look you over. This can be just a fishing expedition or can lead (if you pass) to the real interview with Mr. or

Ms. Big. Make no mistake in thinking that the initial talk session requires no preparation. And despite that bright résumé, remember, you still have to rehearse that *second-act scene* with the leading actor before you play it.

Preparation holds the key to your facility in handling any contingencies. Consider it just as urgent to chart your interview as it would be to prepare for a formal speech.

With the central theme of "What am I trying to accomplish?" *make an outline* of the course you'd like this upcoming conversation-with-a-purpose to take. While the real situation frequently will not follow your plan, the outline (memorized) will serve as a guide to help you stay on the track. Besides, with the script in your head, you'll have the confidence to improvise.

The interviewer generally follows two basic tactical approaches (sometimes combined): the straight *question-and-answer routine* and *the friendly talk* without apparent design.

The simple "they-ask-and-you-answer" approach calls for brief, to-the-point replies. The ability to distinguish between trivia ("I was captain of the softball team") and what matters ("I majored in mechanical drawing") makes you a canny interviewee. You manage also to maneuver the discussion away from time-wasting talk to the business at hand; it can prosper only by *focusing attention on the essentials.*

The informal interview, with relaxed style that seems to lack structure, works better than one-way questions and answers. With the easing of barriers, you are encouraged to share the initiative in the conversation and talk more freely about your interests and aspirations. The man or woman on the other side of the desk also gains the advantage of more instant insight into your character and personality.

While this free-form exploration appears to be without concrete purpose, you'd better stay sharp—*the purpose is there.* If you give the same attention to *listening* as to speaking, you should be able to discern the underlying job objective. Once you do, begin *motivating* your remarks accordingly. "My experience as a researcher in audience analysis should be valuable in your new TV project."

Problem interviewers. You may have to confront one or all of these:

—*The gruff, all-business, crusty type.* If this one gives off bad
vibes, pour on the sugar and kill him (or her) with kindness. Above all,
don't try to win any arguments.

—*The inept, skill-less type.* Take over the discussion tactfully;
here's where your homework pays off. You must second-guess this
questioner and keep a steady eye on the goal.

—*The mum, taciturn type.* You'll have to be a mind reader.
Though the queries may be sparse, your answers must be full and
responsive. Don't be surprised if this type's the one to come up with
the favorable answer.

More often than not, however, your interviewers will display
considerable skill to match their affability. Then, just stay with the
script and play the scene for all it's worth.

Women have long held important positions in the personnel de-
partments of industry, education, and the public services. The greater
numbers who are presently entering the field should bring to their
jobs the ingrained talent that many women have for reaching people.
A feeling for immediacy of contact and a sympathetic, approachable
attitude will always enrich the conversation/interview.

The more skillful the interviewer, the more successful the interview. The good job counselor sets her sights at maintaining a low rate
of turnover. She actively promotes frank and agreeable cooperation,
recognizes applicants as individuals, not stereotypes, and at all times
acts the role of a friendly judge, not a critic. *Attention:* The new
personnel worker (and the experienced one, too) is obliged to upgrade
her speech skills by constant awareness and practice.

Story Line—A Personal History

Susan Composite, job applicant, is under twenty or over
forty-five, not yet married or maybe a grandmother, a first-
time worker or second-career-bound after raising a family.
How does our combination Susan prepare herself for an interview? She believes that to count on the inspiration of the
moment is a foolish gamble. So . . .

Susan begins at the beginning by writing the *story of her*

life—not a cut-and-dried listing as in a résumé. She "lets it all hang out" as her autobiography probes the early years—neighborhoods, schools from sandbox to campus green, friendships (passing and lasting), (paid) lessons on the flute, in modern dance, in judo.

The teenage-acquired skills—working in metal sculpture, designing her own clothes, cross-country skiing, painting (walls, mainly), and constructing bird shelters—have all stayed with her. Her do-goodness shows up in the summer counseling at camps for underprivileged children, canvassing with petitions in hand, stumping for her aunt's congressional campaign.

Susan also recalls the books she has read and reread, the plays and films that moved her, the wide range of music she enjoys—and the people. As her typewriter clicks away, the retrospective view takes on the tinge of her philosophy.

The self-searching on paper grows into a re-creation of herself, helping to clarify and focus her perspectives. By providing the heart of her story, she is ready for the skeleton of her résumé. Finally, Susan delivers *Story Line* aloud, adding the dimensions of voice and emotion to her recital.

Like Susan, your own autobiographical-literary-reading-aloud effort has freed your spirit and/or psyche; it's time now to turn to a bread-and-butter investigation of job and career.

Are you one of the lucky women who knew early in life what she wanted to do and did it? Or are you: a recent college graduate with unfocused goals? an office-wife, bound to a dull job with no future? a job-returnee who fears her skills are outdated? a well-established professional seeking new challenges?

Then back to the typewriter for a serious self-quiz to weigh your place in the working world. How would you answer these and similar relevant questions:

What general career areas are best suited to my talents?

Am I willing to travel or relocate?

Do I need a refresher of my work skills or a retraining program?

How can I implement my current job and work toward advancement?

How do my career interests and family needs fit together?

As a professional, should I switch from corporate into private practice?

Does my speaking call for some refurbishing—should I enroll in a speech improvement course, join a speech workshop, or consult a private teacher?

Creating a creative résumé. Tailor yours to suit your needs; *target it* for the specific job; *particularize it* by pointing up your strengths; *personalize it* with pertinent "who, what, where, and when" data; *dramatize it* by adding the "why," an individual account of successful problem solving; *summarize it* with your life's achievements and ambitions; *decorate it* with honors, awards, or grants you have won; *revise it* until it's edited clean; and *make it look good* by faultless typing on spotless paper, limited to one or two pages.

Have you a sketchy work history? Then pad the résumé with your educational background (and those latest extension courses), highlight your experiences in community and civic affairs: the leadership roles and volunteer work in health care, ecology, fund-raising or politics. Remember that in organizing people, in solving problems, in raising funds, and in making strong, motivating talks to groups or stimulating speeches before audiences, you have been building serviceable and salable skills.

For added know-how: The Women's Bureau, Workplace Standards Administration, U.S. Department of Labor, Washington, D.C. 20210, dispenses the latest information concerning women at work. Send for their listings of publications (there may be a small charge). The U.S. Government Printing Office, Public Documents Department, Washington, D.C. 20402, also provides listings of varied materials of interest to women.

Some Concise Advice

You can adapt the techniques for the employment encounter to many other areas: research projects, graduate-school applications, fund-raising, campaigning, and casework.

1. *Make a company profile.* Do your homework on the significant features of the firms you might want to join—company size, subdivisions, products, services. (Check company's P.R. department for

stockholders' reports and company brochures, and the public library for business directories, trade journals, etc.) Weed out unlikely prospects and once you've narrowed your choice to a likely one, get a line on the particular interviewers, if you can.

Important: Look into the firm's *employment policy toward women:* are women eligible for training programs, are there openings for women in nontraditional positions, are there women executives? To become informed about fair employment practices, check with your state's Division of Human Rights.

2. *Trial by voice.* Nasality, whispery nontones, and pronounced localisms turn interviewers off. Do you practice with your cassette the night before? When finally "on stage," you shouldn't think about your speech but concentrate instead on the big scene.

3. *Dressing the part.* Make sure you don't look like a model unless you're seeking a modeling job. Watch your makeup (the length of your false lashes and the green eye shadow). If you like the easy stance you have in pants, choose a nicely tailored slacks suit. Above all, wear what you look good in.

4. *Rehearsing the script.* Role playing is a widely used technique in many professions and businesses; why not put it to use yourself? Find a willing friend or perhaps a member of your family and act out your interview. It's surprising how often this will clarify the twists and turns of the imminent for-real scene. A sharp stand-in might ask, "What makes you think with your lack of experience you can fill the position?" and other such posers to test your equilibrium for come-what-may.

5. *The trick and other questions.* Watch being trapped into tangents by an open-endedquery like "What is your *ideal* job?" Answer forthrightly, "A job that measures up to my education and background." Your replies to specific questions (based on the résumé) should be in terms of *your achievements* rather than in bland dates and places.

6. *The need and the benefit.* Try to get the interviewer to do the talking, especially to point up the company's particular need so you can come back with how *you* can benefit *them.* "I *know* I can fill the position because . . ."

7. *Fasten your headset.* Brush up listening skills by reviewing the three interrelated actions that add up to active response (p. 115). While

the questioners have the floor (make sure you let *them* talk!), hang on to what is said and especially to what *isn't*.

8. *The résumé doesn't say how well you did.* Fill in with concrete illustrations: "I saved C. Brown, Inc., $10,000 on the last government contract." Or, if you have something to show, do so: "Would you like to see my blueprints for the new recreation hall?" To the visual aids (including yourself), add the plus of attractive tone, clear enunciation, and an ease with words.

9. *Can you type?* When asked, do you come out fighting? This once legitimate question has come to mean a put-down for many a qualified and aspiring woman. *But*—a novice on the job market may have to begin as a minor secretary. Besides, many women (and now increasing numbers of men) in secretarial posts have executive status with commensurate pay.

10. *Knock the chip off.* If you begin to bristle at some point in the conversation, cool it. Rather turn your anger toward objectivity by considering the motivation behind your interviewer's remark. Concede and agree as much as you can with dignity, presenting your own position fairly and *pleasantly*.

11. *"Excuse me a moment."* When the discussion is interrupted by a telephone call or other intrusion, hold on to what was last said. When the interview resumes you can then paraphrase smoothly the words that were cut off: "You were saying, Mr. Wilson, that . . ."

12. *Hold these truths.* Laws establishing women's rights to equal treatment in employment have been on the books for some time now. Today, illegal questions include those referring to age, marital status, race, and religion. In an interview, however, you can't, when asked one of these, just declare, "That's illegal!" unless you're prepared to head for the door. You may prefer instead to work deftly around the question. When you've landed the job, you can find allies among the other women employees, and together begin to affirm your rights.

On the Scene

Now let's see how all of the foregoing adds up. Susan Composite, who wrote her autobiography for us on p. 132, is now the leading lady (not the ingénue) in this scene with an employer/interviewer. If she appears to know all the answers, it's because she exemplifies all our eager job applicants rolled into one. She has prepared herself rigorously for this moment of truth.

The scene opens with Mr. Amalgamate, V.P. in charge of recruitment, seated at his rococo fruitwood desk. He rises as his status British receptionist enters to announce crisply in her overseas accent that Ms. Composite has arrived. Susan makes her entrance with a confident stride and her smile, hairdo, makeup, outfit, are all understated. Mr. Amalgamate extends his hand, she shakes it readily and says in her good American speech, "Good morning, Mr. Amalgamate, I've looked forward to meeting you."

He measures her with a discerning glance; his manner is urbane and inscrutable. "Good morning, Miss Composite, please sit down," he says, and motions her to the chair on the other side of the desk. She seats herself, both feet securely on the floor. They begin the encounter with pleasantries; Susan, a practiced conversationalist, responds with an on-her-toes alertness. But the friendly give-and-take clearly has an underlying purpose—friendly yes, cozy no. "What a magnificent view," Susan remarks. Amalgamate comments, "Yes, it's great until the elevators break down."

As the poker-faced executive studies her résumé, Susan reminds herself that while he appears to hold all the aces (including her job), she's there because the company needs to fill that job. She has come armed with answers (rehearsed) for whatever questions may come her way. Susan Composite has applied for the job of: administrative assistant/computer programmer/office manager/engineer (industrial, architectural, chemical, or packaging).

Our leading lady makes a point of name-dropping (especially his). She memorizes names and handles them with ease; she inserts his in her remarks: "Oh, of course, Mr. Amalgamate," also adding, "Your receptionist, Ms. Smythe, explained that . . ."

Susan tunes in on even the smallest detail of their discussion; she has developed the impressive ability of referring to The Other's remarks in hers. She proceeds smoothly, "If, as you've outlined, Mr. Amalgamate, *Data Processing* coordinates 37 per cent of the work allotted the fifteen subdivisions for *final processing,* do you think perhaps I might fit into *distribution planning?*"

Susan directs her pleasing voice toward the listener, never permitting her words to go astray (her eyes on his face, *not* on a spot over his head). Her enunciation is clear and unaffected, for the skilled listener always sees through artificiality. Susan avoids answering in monosyllables; a short yes or no sounds inarticulate and can be a dead end. "Yes—I love to bicycle in the park on weekends . . ."

She adroitly works her way around some of the more difficult, sometimes trick questions. For a starter, Mr. Amalgamate suggests nonchalantly, "Tell me *all* about yourself." Susan responds, "You have the vital statistics in hand, sir . . . I should like to mention some of the immodest omissions. I took honors in art [or speech, music, theater, languages, etc.], and at Ohio State I was awarded this watch with an inscription at graduation." She holds it up briefly. "Also, I've taken the liberty of bringing an article from the Cleveland *Plain Dealer* about the competition I won in forensics [or the French horn, or the set designs for the Community Playhouse]."

She's prepared for "How much money do you expect?" and she counters with "What is the salary range for the job?" "Well, Miss Composite," he pursues, "what do *you* think you're worth?" She manages that one with, "I think, Mr. Amalgamate, that I'm worth a great deal. But I'll be guided by *your* estimate of my talents."

He suddenly pops this one, "What did you do in the years between 1968 and 1970?" Susan, who has purposely omitted those years (a private matter) from her résumé, doesn't become flustered. She keeps her cool. "I took time out to visit my aunt in Australia and then toured the Far East." (The reason could have been a sick child, a broken love affair, or an artistic sabbatical.)

"Are you married, Miss Composite?" doesn't throw her either. She answers with a smile, "You know, Mr. Amalgamate, I really shouldn't answer that, especially since your company has a government contract and would want to abide by the laws." His retort is quick, "Oh, you must be one of those women's libbers!" Susan replies tactfully, "I do believe in the equality of rights and opportunities for *men and women.*"

The Other raises an eyebrow, "I just wanted to know what you'd do if your husband's job were transferred." Susan pours on the sincerity: "Believe me, Mr. Amalgamate, I'm not trying to mislead you . . . I love my home and leaving it is just not in the cards."

This time *he* smiles. "Actually, Miss Composite, our company welcomes housewives returning to work, since we consider them stable employees. So if you plan to raise a family, we'd welcome you back afterward." Responsive to this display of sentiment, Susan declares frankly, "I appreciate very much your company's attitude. My goal, however, at this point, is to pursue my career."

After that last exchange, an atmosphere of greater relaxation and mutual respect pervades the conversation. The employer/interviewer gets down to the actual business of the interview by delineating the company's requirements for the specific opening. While we cannot crystal-gaze the final outcome, there can be no doubt that Susan makes an excellent impression.

Concluding the interview, the executive leads Susan to the door: "Thank you for coming, *Ms.* Composite, it was a pleasure." Susan doesn't delay her departure and extends her hand, her clasp perhaps somewhat warmer than when she arrived. She speaks her exit lines with assurance, "Thank you, Mr. Amalgamate, for the time you gave me. I should like to work on Consolidated Incorporated's new aerospace project—I trust *your* department will consider me for the position of programmer." As she moves through the outer office, Susan remembers the British receptionist: "Thank you, Ms. Smythe, very much."

As Susan returns home, she immediately writes out all she can remember of the interview dialogue (to be examined critically in preparation for the next contest in the job arena). How Susan talked, walked, stood, sat, and kept her face expressive made up the whole of what she had communicated. First and last, her winning voice spoke for her.

The woman who values her speech, putting it to use in the service of essential self-expression, makes the most able communicator. Unfortunately, personnel directors judge people, and especially women, on the basis of voice stereotypes. They rarely wait to discover the genuine capabilities beneath the mousy or strident voice. "She's not the type" means, nine times out of ten, "I don't like the way she sounds." In a period of economic bind, good speaking can make the difference.

Unlike the interview, where the purpose may be only implied, and unlike conversation which rarely stays with a topic, the *conference* and other *group forms* (next in order) have a *specific* intention and discussion is *sustained.*

9

Dynamics of Discussion

Probably no other country has produced such a web of organizations, societies, clubs, and committees—Americans in infinite grass-roots congresses—discussing, deliberating, disputing, and deciding.

Within this historic gathering into groups, women have played a key role and through the years have gone right on exercising and refining the fine art of organizing. Everywhere that women come together in cooperative effort, the accumulated wisdom of democratic decision-making and of devotion to the common good is plainly visible.

It was the custom only yesterday to poke fun at clubwomen; cartoons of large-busted women in funny hats still turn up in some newspapers and magazines. (They should know better!) It is time at last to stop laughing at the women who have contributed enduringly to our life and times.

Together with purpose. In and out of schools we find misplaced emphasis on the glamorous one-person-talks-while-others-listen delivery—known otherwise as public speaking. More suitable, useful, and important to our life-styles is the reasoning together of a small body of people with a more or less common cause.

Relatively few women will ever face a large audience, though many of them participate regularly in business conferences, staff meetings, caucuses, executive boards, and committees, and in the multiform groups devoted to study, politics, therapy, sports, fundraising, and consciousness-raising.

These diverse groups, based as they are on structured conversation, obviously offer rich dividends in improved speech. Does your

140

mind need stretching, also your voice and vocabulary? Then do your homework to prepare yourself for the next staff meeting or study group. The gains you make in fluency and self-expressiveness will feed back into all areas of daily living.

Some ground rules and how-to's. Excerpted from the definition of the word *discuss* (Webster's Third New International Dictionary, Unabridged):

> *Discuss:* To converse or talk about: exchange views or information about ... DISCUSS implies a reasoned conversational examining, esp. by considering pros and cons, in an attempt to clarify or settle.

This definition underscores the difference between merely conversing about something and seriously investigating all sides of a question. Let us say, for example, that when two women discuss the merits or demerits of the posh Texas emporium Neiman Marcus, they're just talking. But if Mr. Neiman and Mr. Marcus discourse together on the same subject—*that's* a discussion! Thus, the conference or group discussion is a cooperative effort to reach a satisfactory meeting of minds, to work toward mutual solutions of a problem.

We—not I or they. When you're troubled about some question and try to go it alone in search of an answer, do your thoughts often seem to run ahead in a jumble? While we still think individually as part of a group, the give-and-take among members can develop a strong bond of interdependent thinking. No longer just a collection of people, a *group* has come into existence—without speeches as in public address, or rebuttals as in formal debate.

Each participant can be first a speaker, then a listener, then again a speaker, and so it should go. As a matter of course, men and women join in business conferences, staff meetings, community drives, and wherever working relationships exist and certain common interests are involved.

The group concept. The process of what is called *group dynamics*, or sometimes *GroupThink*, cannot flourish without careful seeding. Its conception springs from a number of people reasoning and working together in cooperative effort. The secret is mathematical—ten people in close conclave do not add up simply to one-plus-one-plus-one (etc.)

equals ten. When the dynamics of interaction operate freely in discussion within a group, the result in quality climbs in *geometric proportion.*

As in baking bread, the ingredients rise *if* you mix them well and *wait.* Time invested in building understanding and democratic function pays off; the pooling of ignorance or the venting of pettinesses is time lost forever.

Do you tend to react subjectively when a pet idea is rejected? But *you* have not been rejected. Change your perspective by turning your feelings outward to bolster the *group concept.* As a member of a team for problem-solving, decision-making, mediation, training, or enlightenment, get on the road, along with your co-workers, and head toward the desired and mutual goal.

Let us now look and listen in on some discussions which take place in a variety of organizations, involving women today. In a series of brief scenes, each ending with a *discussion rule,* we shall determine what went wrong. Taken together, these rules form a ready reference for effective group functioning.

1. Problems, Problems

The Setting: The Hands of Women, Inc., a suburban crafts shop crowded with sculpture, pottery, stained glass, and macramé. Female-owned, -operated, and -crafted.

The Scene: A business meeting of the cooperative, discussing whether to relocate the shop to larger quarters.

An "adorable" studio has been found and the women enthuse over decorating the new place; they'll paint murals, design built-in furniture, and hang original mobiles from the ceiling. Finally, they get down to the nitty-gritty of problems: the high rent, the studio is four flights up with no elevator or parking facilities and probably cooking odors from the restaurant below.

"Well," the coop's bookkeeper opines, "I guess we'd better start all over again and decide *first* what kind of space would be best for us."

Discussion Rule #1: Begin by focusing on the problem, not on the solution. If you rush to a conclusion, you'll have to rethink the problem. Batting an idea around in a group may seem to be time-consuming but usually turns out to be time-saving and a productive procedure.

2. Here We Come

The Setting: The club car of the Metroliner on the Washington, D.C., run of the Penn Central RR.

The Scene: The lobbying committee of the Philadelphia League of Women Voters on their way to the capital to lobby in the Senate for ratification of the Equal Rights Amendment.

Even with the subdued rumble of this crack train, some of the women cannot be heard at all—the current of their talk appears to be directed inward rather than outward. Their most persuasive attributes—the transcendent good will, enthusiasm, and keen know-how—do not always come through the personal barriers. The women admonish and bolster each other. "Now, Carol, no mumbling." "Edith, you're talking through your nose again." "What *did* you say, Doris?" "Ann, look out, you're becoming strident."

While making assignments, the lobbying committee continues "putting it on the line." "Senator Wurst will love your soft-sell approach, but be sure he *hears* you!" "When you tone down, you'll be great for Senator Ruffman, he's our toughest nut to crack." "*Will* you cut out your *ain'ts,* the Southern bloc won't cotton to them—they appreciate the 'well-turned phrase.' "

Discussion Rule #2: Keep uppermost in mind the desire to communicate. **Do you *want* to be heard and believed? Learn by doing; don't wait for full-blown results. Your live contacts with people will release the constraints. Keep brushing up skills of voice, vocabulary, and conversation (and don't overlook body language). Do some role-playing *in advance* of every important scene —if you can convince your friends, everyone else will be easier.**

3. I'm Right—You're Wrong

The Setting: A meeting room off the rectory of a church in a Midwestern city.

The Scene: A group of twenty women, seated around a refectory table, in a meeting organized by the St. Joanites and the Rachelites, an interfaith committee.

The organizers seek to achieve greater equality for women within the orthodoxy of church and temple. To enlist their influence in liberalizing ecclesiastical ritual, prominent women from different faiths have been invited as guests.

An emotional argument erupts as the St. Joanites call for rejection of the present submissive wife-to-husband rites, and demand "equal rites" within the church. They are supported by the Rachelites, who also protest the segregation of the sexes in the synagogue and the men's morning prayer thanking God for not being born a woman.

An irate voice proclaims, "But a wife is a queen in a Jewish household!" Another chimes in, "The Mother of God is revered by all!" The organizers attempt to calm the atmosphere with a rational statement of principles, but to no avail. Some of the guests, refusing to listen, leave and the meeting breaks up.

Discussion Rule #3: *Cultivate an attitude of open-mindedness* and the desire to understand the views and beliefs of others. We tend to vindicate ourselves instead of verifying facts; "You're right and I'm wrong" is hard to admit. Among the seven deadly sins listed in the Middle Ages was self-justification.

4. Hear, Hear

The Setting: A conference room at the local Y in Sharon, Pennsylvania, the weekly gathering place of Community Consumers in Action.

The Scene: A meeting, consisting mainly of women, listening to the report from the dietitian of Sharon General Hospital, who heads their steering committee.

"At our last meeting, we discussed conducting a house-to-house survey on consumers' reactions to unit pricing of food products. [At this point one woman, having registered the word *survey,* stops listening and pursues her own thoughts.] Since then we received the state's latest report on the effect of unit pricing."

The dietitian continues, "Therefore, we propose instead that the members report to the next meeting on management follow-through of these new government regulations at the supermarket level." The woman who hasn't been listening speaks up: "I don't think we should have a house-to-house survey; it takes too much time. Besides, it's too cold at this time of year, and it seems to me that—"

The dietitian breaks in with, "You must have misunderstood,

Clara, we have already decided to *drop* the survey . . ." The other women stare at Clara without a word. The discussion has been unexpectedly stalled.

Discussion Rule #4: Listen efficiently; keep testing your recall. If you stop attending to a speaker, do you merely smile, nod, and pretend to have heard it all? Strive for good ear memory—practice by restating as much as you can of what's been said. Poor listening cuts down reaction and interaction, the very life of group discussion.

5. If at First . . .

The Setting: An empty garage, set up as campaign headquarters in a small farming community in South Dakota.

The Scene: A meeting of the committee (four men, five women) for the election of Maude Barton to the State Senate.

Though they all vote conscientiously each year, these grass-rooters have little experience in political organization. One of the younger men, currently in graduate school, who is therefore deemed best choice for chairman, becomes an instant expert in procedure. A stickler for Robert's Rules of Order, he calls for motions and votes, and forms committees within committees—all in formal parliamentary language. "Do I hear a motion to amend the main motion that the campaign literature distribution committee should be limited to eight? And is there a second to the motion?"

Everyone feels constrained and awkward, interaction within the group approaches zero, and little work is accomplished. The committee dies aborning.

Discussion Rule #5: Follow the informal procedure of group discussion: leadership that guides rather than dictates, give-and-take between members, encouraging people to speak, and promoting interpersonal relationships—in a relaxed atmosphere devoid of parliamentary formalisms and unnecessary flourishes.

6. Even Jellyfish Have Structure

The Setting: A floor-through brownstone apartment on Manhattan's East Side.

The Scene: A gathering of One-Parent Ltd., recently formed by individual parents with children—divorced women and men, widows and widowers—and the "new singles" with adopted children.

The bimonthly meetings ponder the mutual problems of single parenthood. On this particular evening the group is considering the problem of enuresis, or bed-wetting. The discussion is as haphazard as the seating arrangement with people perched on arms of chairs or settled on the floor.

Apparently, these parents have a higher percentage of bed-wetters (aged five to twelve) than other families—or so they think. They attribute this condition to the lack of a second parent with a consequent lack of security in the child. A young mother blurts out, "But many children have this problem *and two parents*—why do we always have to blame ourselves?"

The talk wanders all around the subject: "Maybe it's organic, not psychological." "The youngsters need the right training, that's all." "Oh, they'll outgrow it." "My Benjie loves salty foods—is that good or bad?" "When Judy wants a Coke or glass of milk before bedtime, should I say no?" "I know a mother who uses a bell device that goes off the minute the sheet gets wet." "That's just awful!" "Why don't we consult a child psychologist?"

And so it goes, the chatter continuing right through coffee-and-cake time. Disenchanted with the aimless proceedings, some prospective members of One-Parent Ltd. leave early. The next meeting is poorly attended.

Discussion Rule #6: Prepare yourself beforehand to contribute to any group meeting. Half-informed members can only reach half-baked decisions. Don't waste time "deciding to decide"—get to it. Nearly any system of preparation is better than none. Save time for the gestation of your thoughts (perhaps when taking a walk or when first awakening in the morning). Organize your ideas, do some research, make outlines—and check with your cassette.

7. The Voice of Unreason

The Setting: An empty store, the temporary headquarters of Black Women United, in a shopping mall outside of Chicago.

The Scene: A group of women, sitting around on improvised furnishings, at a meeting called by the membership committee.

The subject under discussion is how to struggle against *racism without and sexism within the black community*. The interchange heats up and becomes personal as antagonisms mount.

"You got no business putting our men down—you've never been married, that's why!" "You're an *Aunt Jemima.*" "*Women's libber* —you're living in a white world, sister!" "All *you* know is frying chicken for church suppers!" "Sure, I do day work—it's better than some of the night work I could think of!"

The voices of reason try to intervene and get back on the track of building a political and economic program for the advancement of black women. But it's rough going.

Discussion Rule #7: Attack issues, not people. Watch the tendency to work out frustration and anger on the group. Regard those who differ with you as co-workers and together promote interpersonal relationships and mutual trust. Though not everyone's opinion is worthy, everyone's is *worthy of attention*. Debaters aim to exploit each other's weaknesses; in true give-and-take discussion, we aim to overcome our own.

8. Time to Speak Up

The Setting: The editorial room of *HerSelf*, a Woman's Newsletter, a new publication, housed in the basement of a Unitarian church in Richmond, Virginia.

The Scene: The editorial board discussing a proposal to add a male journalist to the all-female staff.

There have been increasing rumblings and grumblings about the antimale slant of *HerSelf* reportage. A minority of the staff has made the proposal to hire a man, hoping thereby to mitigate the extremism of the majority. In the face of strong and voluble opposition, however, the minority crumbles and offers little support for its own proposal. It is defeated without a dissenting vote.

In a post-mortem discussion by the losers, one of them moans, "Why didn't we make a fight for it—*it was the right idea!*"

Discussion Rule #8: Resist the pressure to conform. A danger within groups is knuckling under to the pressure of majority opinion. Women too insecure to express opposition will tell their intimate friends how they feel *after* the

board meeting. A good approach for groups is to make a rule to hear all minority opinions. Remember, many an idea is conceived in a minority of one.

9. The Drag of the Past

The Setting: The living room of an apartment in a condominium housing development in the city of Detroit.

The Scene: A meeting of the organizing committee of WISH (Women Inc. for Shorter Hours) for the purpose of enlisting neighborhood women to collect names on petitions for a thirty-hour work week referendum.

As the committee members hand out the petitions, they engage the women in a discussion of WISH's challenge to the conventional working day. They point out that the concept of the eight-hour day is not sacred—only fifty years ago it was considered radical, and before that, the ten-hour day.

For working mothers, eight hours a day on a job plus running a household is thoroughly exhausting. Shorter hours would also enable fathers to share more of the family responsibilities and to enjoy their children.

The neighborhood women raise immediate objections. "No, the change in hours would upset everything—women are accustomed to the eight-hour day." "Men don't have the patience to take care of children, and you can't trust them to do the shopping." "Besides, shorter hours would shorten profits, too [and this is the clincher], and the whole idea sounds socialistic anyway . . ." Six of the women put down their petitions and bow out.

Discussion Rule #9: Avoid clinging to familiar and traditional thinking. One of the barriers to mental freedom and progress is the need to burrow for safety into the comfortably familiar practices of the past. To investigate new directions takes effort and no little courage.

10. Questions and Answers

The Setting: A classroom of a junior high school in Kenosha, Wisconsin.

The Scene: The regular monthly open house for PTA parents, visiting the school.

The math teacher, seated in her usual place behind the desk, presides. The urgent question of an after-school program comes up. A concerned mother and mainstay of the PTA launches the discussion: "As you know, the police have reported that the use of marijuana has increased in the junior high. We must find ways to keep our children busy over the weekends, and I propose that we plan a Saturday cultural and sports program. Let's have some questions."

"What makes you think the police report is accurate?" a father asks with authority. The resonant masculine voice dominates and the others echo, "I'm sure it's an exaggeration." "It must be." "That's so . . ."

The teacher responds, *"This is a question of fact.* The police have the facts and the State Committee Report backs them up." The parents then decide that obviously the culprits belong to a delinquent minority (not *their* children).

"Let's go back to the Saturday program. What about afternoon piano, dancing, ice skating, and skiing lessons and supervised evening dances with a live band?"

The majority rejects the plan as too elaborate and expensive. "But the Lake Mendota Day School has just such a program." "Hilda, where is your sense of values? How can you compare ours to a rich private school?" Hilda makes no answer to this reproof from her husband.

Comes the final question of policy: which children in the ninth grade should be included in the program? The math teacher interjects quietly, "The school cannot be part of any project that might exclude students." A parent breaks in, "But we can't have that crowd that busses in from the other side of town—it makes no sense. That's actually what we wanted to avoid."

Still arguing, the parents leave—the Saturday program still unresolved and probably to be abandoned.

Discussion Rule #10: Ask the right questions to find the answers. A question, posed correctly, can be more important than knowing the answer. A productive discussion moves efficiently among four broad question types:

questions of verifiable fact (these are not discussable), *questions of interpretation* (translating a fact or set of facts), *questions of value* (assessments of comparative merit or worth), and *questions of policy* (definitions of serious aims and goals). These four basic questions (often combined) form a solid basis for logical and persuasive speaking. In the mutual search for answers to group problems, learn to identify the questions and to spot the weaknesses which may be hidden beneath the cover of language.

11. Words, Words, Words

The Setting: A private hotel dining room in a large suburban town west of Sacramento, California.

The Scene: A joint luncheon meeting of committees for the yearly community fund-raising drive, representing different strata of the town's population.

The meeting gets under way after the dishes are cleared. This year's chairman, a retired physician, calls for subcommittee reports on planned projects for the drive: bazaars, thrift shops, art sales, dances, a formal ball, and sports events, among others. The discussion grows livelier as objections to projects are voiced.

With an inexperienced chairman at the controls, people speak out of turn and often at cross purposes. Acid interchanges spring from the permissive procedure; words, tossed about loosely, cause antagonisms to simmer.

"What do you mean, thrift-shop *merchandise?* Who'll buy that junk?"

"By merchandise *I* mean brand-new clothes donated by a wholesaler."

"Our art sale will exhibit the latest abstractions."

"Oh, you mean those pictures that look like a child did them?"

"Working with a committee is a waste of time. I'd rather do the job myself."

"Mister, don't bite off more than you can chew."

"I'm against a high school dance—those *longhairs* smoking pot and who knows what else."

"Listen to Archie Bunker."

"That so? Then if you ask *me*, women are *dingbats* at planning sports events."

Others pour it on: *"Reactionary . . ." "Idiotic . . ."*

The physician-chairman, who has been rapping for order, raises his voice: "Ladies and gentlemen, *please.* Remember, *united we stand, divided we fall!"*

Discussion Rule #11: Do not assume that because you use a word, the listener shares your meaning. A word arouses images in us as it relates to our experience and imagination; misunderstandings arise when people suppose they both have the same idea in mind. A classic story illustrates:

"Mommy," Sally asks, "where do I come from?" Mommy, somewhat shaken, sits down and takes off with the routine of the birds and the bees. "Oh," Sally muses, "I just wanted to know 'cause Janie comes from Los Angeles."

Watch out for the *word-stoppers*, those that impede the flow of rational talk: *name-calling*, the labels that stab at reason, the contagious *clichés* that pass for wisdom, and the *"finality" statements* of closed minds. Other poor discussion tools: ambiguous remarks and vague concepts going nowhere. Batten words down—*particularize* them. If your ear picks up ambiguous signals from someone, ask for a paraphrase. And, better still, ask for an example.

As we fade out on the last of the scenarios with a message, we turn to the rules of discussion, so sadly slighted by the performers who enacted for us the vexations and dilemmas of committee life. To fix these criteria for good discussion in your mind, let us utilize them as a basis for a rating sheet.

Try this *self-evaluation quiz* after your next meeting (and after subsequent ones); check your performance on each of the rules. After answering the questions, grade yourself *OK* or *NG.* Then, giving yourself five points for each OK, add up the score. A total of 85 and over is very good.

1. *Begin by focusing on the problem, not on the solution.*

   Did I have a clear idea of the basic problems?   OK ☐ NG ☐

   Did I just come up with some snappy solutions before I understood the problem?   OK ☐ NG ☐

2. *Keep uppermost in mind the desire to communicate.*

   Did I get through to the listener?   OK ☐ NG ☐

   Did I speak up or just mumble?   OK ☐ NG ☐

3. *Cultivate an attitude of open-mindedness.*

   Did I attend alertly to others' opinions or did I just stick to my own?   OK ☐ NG ☐

4. *Listen efficiently; keep testing your recall.*

   Did I really listen or did my mind wander?   OK ☐ NG ☐

   Was I able to restate some of the important ideas?   OK ☐ NG ☐

5. *Follow the informal procedure of group discussion.*

   Did the leader keep the meeting on the track without "taking over"?   OK ☐ NG ☐

   Did the group get too bogged down in procedure and obscure the issues?   OK ☐ NG ☐

6. *Prepare yourself beforehand to contribute to any group meeting.*

   Was my advance reading adequate for the scope of the subject?   OK ☐ NG ☐

   Should I have made an outline?   OK ☐ NG ☐

7. *Attack issues, not people.*

   Was I guilty of the tendency to stereotype women and thus, dismiss what they said?   OK ☐ NG ☐

   Did I become somewhat personal when I disagreed with someone, and did it show in my tone of voice?   OK ☐ NG ☐

8. *Resist the pressure to conform.*

   Did I make a stand for my opinions and beliefs, or just let the others intimidate me?   OK ☐ NG ☐

9. *Avoid clinging to familiar and traditional thinking.*

   Do I tend to hesitate to break with established custom?   OK ☐ NG ☐

   Did I reject that idea just because it was new?   OK ☐ NG ☐

10. *Ask the right questions to find the answers.*

Did I phrase questions correctly to encourage
responsive answers?   OK ☐   NG ☐

Was I able to hit the key questions when we were
hammering out a policy for the group?   OK ☐   NG ☐

11. *Do not assume that because you use a word, the*
listener shares your meaning.

Did I make clear statements or were they too
vague to add anything to the discussion?   OK ☐   NG ☐

Did I choose words carefully or just fall back on
clichés?   OK ☐   NG ☐

Did we argue at cross purposes when actually
there was basic agreement?   OK ☐   NG ☐

The new study groups mainly about and for women. Women have
been going to school for a long time—completing at last the post-
poned degrees, flocking to adult education courses, and organizing
political study groups everywhere. This learning drive has greatly
accelerated the education and training of women for business and the
professions. And today's courses, in and out of school, offer a
sweeping range of subjects with provocative titles:

> Making It in a Man's World
> Women and Affirmative Action
> Child, Family, Community
> Human Sexuality
> Women in American History
> Women in Contemporary Society
> The Psychology of the Female Personality

That old homily embroidered into framed samplers, "Give and ye
shall receive," applies anew to the classroom. If you sit there like a
log, you learn little and contribute less. Aren't you also apt to blame
the *dull* instructor, the *boring* textbooks and students? If you put the
discussion rules to work, they will operate in any classroom to lift the
doldrums. And if you consider every course a course in speech as well,
just watch yours improve.

The rise of consciousness-raising. The CR groups, a new fount of
interpersonal communication among women, have been sprouting up

throughout the country. Large numbers of women are garnering comfort and self-knowledge from this leaderless, free, self-regulating process in human relations. Here is an excerpt from a recent illuminating essay on the subject.

Consciousness-raising is a technique in which women tell their own stories—testify, as it were—so that from their common experience they can distill new truths. The key words in consciousness-raising are "the personal becomes political." The personal experiences of each woman are the *facts* that form the basis of her recognition of and insight into the state of women in general . . .

Each member speaks in turn, which gives the shyest a chance to develop and to overcome fears, controls the more talkative, and teaches women to listen to one another. There is a place in consciousness-raising for each woman. Women —young, old, middle-aged—cross lines and find common denominators. "Women's talk," which has traditionally been degraded, is found to be a source of comfort, strength, and insight.

—*The New York Woman's Directory*

10

The Panel: Extended Group
Discussion

For small groups, there is no more congenial setting than the *round table*, a term we have come to associate with *discussion*. For gatherings of forty or more, the appropriate setting of the *panel forum* is an arc or V seating pattern, usually on a platform, to enable the group of panelists to see each other and be seen by an audience.

The members of a panel should number no fewer than three and no more than ten—large enough to include a variety of opinions on a shared subject yet small enough for informal interchange among them and later, with those out front.

Much of the talk on TV and radio comes to the home audience in a familiar panel form; it is on the community level, however, that women should encourage more face-to-face open forums where they can be participants rather than just viewers. In fact, a thought-provoking topic on TV can spark a local cultural or political group to explore the subject further in a panel of their own.

Getting it together. The program committee (practically always composed of women) goes to work organizing the panel. First comes the topic, which can be picked nowadays from a seemingly bottomless barrel of pertinent, lively, and, above all, discussable subjects. The committee then looks about for the panel members who can represent various areas of expertise in the chosen topic. They need not be "names"; one can generally flush a likely candidate from a university, the news media, local government, or even the UN. In any case, the selection should come early enough to allow for preparation (the panel members' and yours).

To help the committee, here are some suggested panel topics of particular interest to women and some prototypes for proposed panelists—all experts with a particular perspective on some important aspect of the coming discussion. These hypothetical choices are all women, for qualified women would be available in every case. Obviously, men also can and do fill such roles.

Panel Topic #1: The Business of Beauty: Trick or Treat?

The Panel Members

A *crusading reporter* talks about the fraudulent claims of ads that mislead; the hyped-up copy with alluring pictures to match—"A gorgeous, sexy young smell ... radiant-looking, baby-smooth ... egg-enriched ... the skin breathes ... Corn Dust, the look of innocence ..."

A *dermatologist.* The potentially harmful ingredients of cosmetics, including hormones—the allergic reactions, itching, scaling, and skin eruptions; the inexpensive generic substitutes available for good skin care.

A *consumer researcher.* The need for stricter federal food and drug regulation of cosmetics, including honest testing and labeling.

A *former top model.* How to make your own cosmetics, including an avocado-banana-strawberry facial, of organic ingredients.

Panel Topic #2: Child Abuse: Community Crisis

The Panel Members

A *pediatrician from Children's Hospital* talks about the reluctance of doctors to report cases and become involved in court procedures.

A *Family Court judge.* The recently established national center for child abuse and neglect. How it can be implemented.

A *child psychologist.* Therapeutic help for parent as well as child: "The battered child of today is the battering parent of tomorrow."

A *supervisor of a social service program.* The new community self-help clinic for disturbed parents and its hot-line for anonymous calls to report suspected cases.

Panel Topic #3: Mysticism, Witchcraft, and Hysteria

The Panel Members

A nun, dean of Mount Mary College for Women, talks about the misunderstood historical role of the church in exorcism and the current fascination with black magic.

A film and literary critic of the Tribune-Times. The spread of novels, films, plays on Satanic possession. [Audience comments from the block-long lines at the latest movie: "So terrifying ... I love horror movies ... you feel contaminated ... a religious experience ... I got sick ... had nightmares."]

A board member of the Society for Psychical Research. An exposé of demonic sound effects in movies and TV—wheezing on mikes, keening sounds at Irish wakes, groaning from scarves pulled tight around necks, cries of pigs driven to market.

A psychiatrist. The hysteria phenomenon (catharsis). Women, the proverbial "witches," as historical victims of superstition.

Panel Topic #4: The New Non-sexist Sexual Woman

The Panel Members

A gynecologist from the famous Lasters and Thompson sex clinic talks about freeing women's sexual anxieties and the role of counseling programs.

A marriage counselor. The dangers to marriage and the family of the new emancipated attitude toward sex.

The leader of a group grope at the California Mountain Institute. Techniques of reaching people and loosening inhibitions through week end encounter sessions.

Author of "Female Sexuality." The liberating enlightenment of today's woman—younger and older. The misplaced emphasis on techniques in sex manuals.

After the selection of panel and panelists, the program committee next "hires a hall" to suit the meeting's needs. On the morning of the event, the P.C. members take care of the readily assembled panel arrangement, see to the mikes, and, placing them strategically, make an extra one available to the audience. On TV, of course, the studio audience always has its own mike, and even a small podium. It's also obviously a good idea to inform the membership ahead of time by mail or by phone about the topic and the panelists.

The Moderator, the Panelist, and the Listener. Like the three-cornered hat, they share an interrelated and important triangle. Their different roles when well performed in tandem will ensure a smooth and spirited discussion.

1. *You as moderator.* Too shy or uptight? Then perhaps you're not ready for the role of leading lady. Continue practicing at the conversational and discussion level. Attend more panels and get on your feet to ask searching questions. If you belong to a speech workshop, so much the better; *work up to moderator.*

If you feel the impulse and the confidence to play the lead, by all mans take the plunge and learn by doing. *The requirements:* a benign air and a very firm hand, clear speech but no speech-making, a strict sense of time without any hesitation at cutting people off who exceed the limit, and an overall efficiency while not appearing to rush things.

Your important duties as umpire. Make your introductions brief and bright, avoiding extended strings of credits; continue throughout to refer to the members of the panel *by name* (the audience tends to forget); keep the flow of talk going forward in democratic and unrehearsed style (though you've met with the panel a week beforehand to set up procedures).

As leader, keep *yourself* out of it, almost never beginning a statement with "I"; allow at least one third of the scheduled time for questions from the audience, prodding them if necessary; coax the timid and call on qualified individuals (some of whom have been planted) to add comments; clarify vague questions and interpret ambiguous statements. Turn for answers to questions to the panelists, who also direct queries to each other.

While enthusiasm is beautiful, too much can disrupt any meeting, especially when questioners take off on ego trips and monopolize the time. Other members of the audience become restless, then speak up impatiently without waiting to be recognized. You call for order (maybe taking off your shoe to pound the table?), but the unruly noise continues. You try once again with big, firm tones through your mike, until you capture the attention of most of the audience.

In this respect, a humorous story can work wonders. With healing laughter from out front, the heavy atmosphere will lift. Try this one, adjusting the joke to the present scene:

"What's the shape of the earth?" asks Judy's teacher. Judy says it is round. "How do you know it is round, Judy?" And Judy replies, "All right, it's square then. I don't wanna start an argument about it."

Then from the moderator, "Some of you may be *squares* out there, and some of you *rounds,* but let's not start an argument about it. Let's get back on the track—we were saying . . ."

If pandemonium persists (fortunately, a rare occurrence), adjourn the meeting, dismiss the panel with apologies, and walk off the platform.

But if all goes as planned, at the conclusion you have the job of pulling together the main threads of the discussion. Do not summarize the ideas point by point; instead, *synthesize* what has been contributed on all sides of the question. In a few sentences, you communicate the gist of the ninety-minute give-and-take discussion.

Include thank-you's to the members of the panel and the audience. Call the meeting at an end when the interest out front is still high. As the old theatrical adage puts it, "Always leave them wanting more."

2. *You as panelist.* If the topic falls within an area of your interests and competence, do not hesitate to join as a panel member. The experience of speaking in an open forum will pay you back double in increased confidence and fluency.

Prepare astutely (you don't have to be told to research the subject and your assignment). Do check the eleven discussion rules since they have direct application to this larger and more exposed discussion. Bring a few notes (previously confided to your cassette); do not, however, expect to read a speech. Tune up your voice in advance and try to tone down distracting blemishes such as rapid tempo, runaway high pitch, careless pronunciation, and excessive *uh-uh-uh's*.

At the panel event. Though individual views may vary widely, this is a *cooperative* venture. Support the moderator; sustain the tenor of the discussion; regard the other members with courtesy and concern. Do guard against running overtime and having to quit just when you're warming up to the big point.

In argument, be prepared to take as well as give. Stay with the voice level you mike-tested at the start. Don't shoot for optimum delivery; instead concentrate mainly on making yourself clear (with careful pauses); listen in depth to your co-panelists and feel, as you speak, the exhilaration of reasoning together and testing for truths.

3. *You as listener.* For a neophyte, the panel forum offers a ready laboratory for speech development. Even if your knees tell you not to, ask a question. Do some thinking and reading beforehand so you know which questions you'd like to see raised and share them with interested friends; don't come in from left field—relate to the continuity of the discussion. Discover that the mixed feelings of fear, relief, and satisfaction will become eventually the single-purpose desire to communicate and to activate others to participate.

If you're an experienced panel-goer, however, your know-how should enliven the meeting and inspire others to stand up and contribute. Regardless of the brilliant specialists on the platform, the dynamics of audience participation will raise every meeting to a higher level of involvement and accomplishment. If you just take in and don't give out, if you've only nodded your head or shaken it, it's not enough. *Speak up.*

The panel pluses. When the threesome of *moderator, panelist,* and *listener* parlay their individual strengths into a successful end result, everybody wins. Participating in panel discussions will invigorate the growth of your speech skills, increase your ability to listen and reason, to discuss and differ, to build vocal and verbal clarity—and fortify you for a leadership role.

11

The Voice of Leadership

A leader, newly active in industry, government, the professions, or the communities, finds it essential to cultivate her management and communication skills. What are some of the qualities of the expressive speaker who has found "room at the top"?

The able communicator. She never talks down to anyone and always gives due credit to others; her good will, immediately responsive, works like a reflex. Unlike a star, she never takes a solo bow without the rest of the cast. During the long, pressured day, she manages to speak in the lower part of her voice range and carefully avoids the upper reaches—your ears tell you who's in control yet you hear nothing aggressive in the tones.

A superb listener, very little escapes her. During conferences, this executive fashions her remarks compactly and to the point, pacing her delivery by emphasis on key words and by lengthening the vowels within them (p. 61); her phrases flow (p. 56) with the right glides and inflections (p. 99).

A constant student of herself, she believes in frequent vocal check-ups *cum* cassette and an ever-freshened vocabulary. An inveterate reader aloud, she likes also to test her visual delivery with a mirror, watching for the facial grimaces or neck tensions that line faces and tighten voices. After she has recorded some inspiring passage (not the stock-market reports) the played-back sound of her own relaxed, resonant tones reassures her.

"I'd never work for a woman." How antiquated that phrase has begun to sound, along with the cliché that if you made it the hard way you turned into a hard-boiled and *unfeminine* boss. Defeats, over-

whelming competition—incessant let-downs and put-downs—shaped yesterday's tough lady. With more and more women now achievers and leaders, there is less room for bitterness.

Unfortunately, we still have with us a vanishing breed of queen bee, the lone woman on an otherwise all-male staff who likes it that way. If women have scratched their way up the ladder, chances are the scratch will show in their voices.

All aspirants to management positions should, of course, be wary of imitating a masculine and unattractive *"let's-get-things-done"* gruffness. Neither should they assume that, to succeed, they have to fall back on feminine wiles (with tones to match). Women must settle for their *wanted selves*—for the reality of who they are—and take their own route to the executive suite.

Born to lead? We tend to hang on to the belief that there exists some mystical quality inherent in leadership—and how lucky for those who have it. In this period of "firsts"—*first* woman bank president in the state of New York, *first* woman head of the National Council of Churches, *first* woman conductor of a major opera company, and *first* woman to give birth to a baby (in a hospital) while serving her term as member of the House of Representatives—present history has proven that leaders are products of experience.

The skills of leadership can be learned. Leaders develop by grappling with problems, coping with realities, and, above all, relying on the collective wisdom of people working together. No one can go it alone in our interdependent world.

The day you are appointed to head a committee *(who, me?)* will be the beginning of your education in leadership. To become a competent leader, you learn to:

—Master a thorough grasp of the particular problems and goals, whether community- or business-related.

—Respect and trust the democratic *group concept*, reserving a special sensitivity toward individuals.

—Never impugn an individual, but stay with the *issues* and out of personal conflicts.

—Guide the talk in terms of constructive ideas and common sense rather than of right and wrong.

—Pull members or co-workers back on the track when they take off on tangents.

—Find the flexibility to make adjustments when things bog down.

—Keep order tactfully by suggesting without formality that members indicate to the chair their desire to speak.

—Set up a list of what should be covered—not a formal agenda to be plowed through.

—Always ask if your list is accurate and adequate or if there are any proposed changes.

—Nurture your speech skills at meetings by careful use of voice and words.

—*And* listen intently to all.

Two minuses. The types of leadership that hamper progress include:

1. *The laissez-faire leader.* She exerts no influence, even on herself. Arriving unprepared to a meeting of staff or committee, she queries, "What's on today's agenda?" She imagines her supine behavior to be ultra-democratic, when actually the effect is runaway anarchy unless some enterprising group spirit takes the reins and rescues the meeting.

2. *The "genius" leader.* At the other extreme, this one carries the whole program on her own shoulders—a pretty risky business since the outcome stands or falls on her star performance. Of course, if the project succeeds, she takes the kudos; if it doesn't, she can always blame the lack of cooperation of other members.

The no-single leadership. This interesting form of group direction demands a committed leader who works hard at motivating *others* to contribute to the general good. She pilots a meeting by picking up faint signals of creativity and initiative and then fanning the individual sparks. Her philosophy: the word *cooperative,* even if repeated endlessly like an incantation, has no magic in itself unless the dynamics of group cooperation come into play.

This apparently directionless guidance, a waiting game for the release of submerged energies and talent, requires supreme self-control and self-effacement from a leader. She must also set a high standard in her pursuit of knowledge and dedication to mutual ideals. As more of the women assume leadership within the group, the goal becomes the responsibility of all. The conclusion: there is no longer a single leader, but the group has splendid and productive leadership.

Perhaps the process grinds too slowly for today's sense of urgency, but the results can prove galvanic in terms of personal enrichment and involvement in fruitful action on many fronts.

Success stories. These capsule case histories are all composites of many similar stories of women who rose from the ranks to leading positions in their special fields. Their advancement grew out of talent and diligence, and particularly out of the creative ability to work with and to encourage others.

All these projects and problems spring from real situations. Their outcome in all cases cannot be neatly wrapped up in a slick success package, for while the women made their mark as leaders, often forces beyond their control made the decisions. The hour-and-a-half staff meetings have been reduced to a few highlighted impressions.

Success Story #1

Profile

Peggy Balance, executive director of Mother Earth Foods, Inc.

M.A. in Home Economics and Dietetics at Iowa State, 1953; former teacher, began business career as assistant nutritionist with Famous Brands, Inc., promoted step by step to present top position in their subsidiary, initiated excellent human relations within the plant; mindful of her own previous feeling of isolation, she has been actively supportive of new female personnel.

Project

Ceres Soys, the soy-bean snack (named by Ms. Balance after the Roman goddess of grain).

Problem

Sales have fallen below expectations and behind the competition's Nutty Soys.

The Staff Meeting

Peggy Balance's approach is not a reproach; she addresses the group as one concerned with a mutual problem. "What have we been doing wrong? Now let us consider what we can do right. Helen, why don't you begin?"

The nutritionist. True, we use no artificial preservatives, but we still use chemical farming. Why not switch to organically grown ingredients more in line with our *Mother* Earth concept?

The copywriter. Organic, that's the magic word—it would spark a new ad campaign.

The production head. Hold on—our price is rock-bottom now. The cost of organic stuff would be out of sight.

The director (Peggy). You're right to worry, Ronald, but Ingrid Gustafsen, who runs a large organic farm near here with her husband, tells me they can meet our price and would like to supply us. John, let's hear from you.

The head of the sales staff. Well, Peggy, we've been pushing Ceres Soys as a snack—with improved quality, we could also offer it as a cereal plus a baking item—a *three-way product.*

The packaging engineer. Great—instead of the old cereal boxes, why couldn't we design small gunny sacks as if they came fresh from a granary?

And so it goes; everyone pitches in with shared enthusiasm until it's time for the director to sum up. "Thank you for your contributions. We have to hold down costs *and* keep to our goal of a superior product—let's try for a big splash in the natural-foods market. Is there anything else to include in our report to the board?"

The outcome

The new Ceres Soys may never reach supermarket shelves, or they may soon be on their way to becoming a household word like Grape-Nuts.

Success Story #2

Profile

Melanie Allen, first woman TV producer of a national network sports program, B.S. in journalism, Tulane University, 1960, won swimming trophy on college team, began as production assistant on local radio (recipe reportage), went on to educational TV (small tots' programs), spent some years as associate producer for public affairs programs. Melanie decided in 1971 that the time had come to speak up for a promotion as full producer or to resign; higher-ups stalled, uncertain of company policy; dilemma was solved when necessity arose to fill producer post on a proposed sports series. She got and held the job.

Project

The presentation of a women's sports special on national television.

Problems

Melanie's precarious position as producer in the male-dominated TV industry. Her immediate concern: to weld a cohesive working team out of the personnel that has been assigned her.

The Production Meeting

The new producer expresses her enthusiasm at the prospect of working with this top-notch staff. There is a fumbling start with some random remarks exchanged. Private thoughts hang in the uneasy air: the associate producer's resentment (she was passed over for Melanie's job), the new production assistant's insecurity, the production secretary's tongue-tied awe, the well-known TV director's indulgent attitude (this "girl wonder" will have to prove herself to *him*).

Melanie, who has picked up the unspoken signals, calls on her patience, fortitude, and skill to pull this nongroup together. Her goal: to involve them all in individually satisfying mutual endeavor. She makes good use of a straightforward, clearly spoken approach: "I think our special should be an all-American women's event. How do the rest of you feel about it?"

The director. I for one don't go for it—the show needs *international names* to compete with the soaps and quizzes—that's all women watch anyway.

Melanie (appeals directly to her brooding associate producer). Ms. Rich, don't you agree that we have our own champions—top female swimmers, gymnasts, golfers, tennis stars, and even winning jockeys?

Ms. Rich (her envy lessening). Certainly—I'm for an American show.

The new production assistant (finding her voice). How about U.S. stars like Billie Jean King, Chris Evert, Judy Rankin, Cathy Rigby . . .

The director. Okay, okay—your idea could be far enough out to be *in!* But, please, let's not go overboard and have women's sports from now on just because you gals are running things.

Melanie. I appreciate your candor, and believe me, the show needs you, Arthur. Let's remember for the record—no one's on the barricades. Who knows—the next time around we may decide on featuring both men and women athletes—not, however, in competition.

Everyone laughs. That does it—with a common, defined goal the staff members help to strengthen the group's resolve and to seat the leader more firmly in the saddle. The sports special is away and running.

The outcome

The All-American Women's Sports Special (a TV first) topped the ratings and Melanie was named producer of four more prime-time specials, or Melanie's show ended up scheduled in the same time slot as another channel's premiere TV showing of the motion picture *The Exorcist!*

Success Story #3

Profile

Beth Motley, newly appointed dean of the Mary McLeod Bethune College in North Carolina, American Negro educator, B.A., Howard University, 1944, M.A. New York City College, 1946, Ph.D. University of Chicago, 1950. A civil libertarian, Beth Motley challenged segregation on an interstate Alabama bus in 1963 and wound up in jail for several days, later led sit-ins at all-white restaurants in Biloxi, Mississippi, sought admission to Yale Law School but was rejected because of her sex. Ms. Motley is a former professor of education at Barnard College, and currently special advisory assistant to the Department of Health, Education, and Welfare in Washington.

Project

To reorganize the faltering Bethune College, a previously segregated black school for women. The dean's goal: to build the college into a coeducational, integrated institution as a positive force for reconciliation in terms of both race and sex. Her role models: Eleanor Roosevelt and Dr. Martin Luther King, Jr.

Problems

To convince educators from various sections of the country to join the faculty; to raise much-needed funds for new dormitories and classrooms from government and private sources; to invite prestigious white community leaders to join with black leaders on the board of trustees.

The Meeting of the Board of Trustees

' Professor Motley conducts the meeting as she once did her classes with an open "What do *you* think?" approach. The members respond freely in a convivial interchange of ideas and differences.

A skeptical undercurrent surfaces. "Don't you think we're going too far in expecting white students to enroll in a black school?" asks a community leader noted for her support of the local hospitals.

Dean Motley's reply is authoritative, yet conciliatory. "I appreciate your concern for the student body. I believe, however, that if we set high standards of scholarship and social action, students of all races will want to join our ranks." She thus expresses her guiding belief: stand up for principles without antagonizing those who might stand in your way.

The Outcome

The Mary M. Bethune College has become an inspiring example of academic and social ideals in the New South, or adequate government and private funds were not forthcoming; faculty "names" did not rally to the school's banner; trustees were immersed in other worthy causes and black students enrolled instead in welcoming Northern universities. The upshot: the college foundered.

Success Story #4

Profile

Three young upper-middle-class women, close friends, form the nucleus of leadership for an outstanding community program in a large suburban town; two are married (one divorced), all have children, one is a former nurse, another a former teacher, and the third attends night school to finish her degree.

Project

The formation of an after-school day care center for less-privileged children of working mothers.

Problems

The three women's initial scheme falls apart—the funding for such an elaborate project would have been enormous. With their second try, they set up a small afternoon program in the back of a store that turns out to be an impractical location. Undaunted, they call a meeting of interested women to take stock of the situation.

The Organizational Meeting

They decide:

To choose a name, the Merry-Go-Round Day Care Center.

To find a center facility in a church with available space.

To organize car pools to transport the youngsters from school to the center.

To make full use of community facilities.

To aim for an enrichment program for the children: dancing classes, dramatics, ice skating, field trips, help with homework (their mothers to pick them up at 6 P.M.).

To bring these children together in a recreational relationship with other community children.

To set up a democratic board of directors in which the program children's parents participate.

The Outcome

A true success story. The suburban public school system, at first uncooperative with Merry-Go-Round, becomes enthusiastic about its dramatic effect on the children's classroom work. It offers the center new headquarters in a school building. Run entirely by volunteers and operating on a shoestring, the center is licensed by the state.

The augmented leadership of ten women engages a professional staff director and two assistants, enlists a core of 150 volunteers, including teenagers, and places 200 more children on the waiting list. Their integrated program is studied and copied by other communities throughout the state. The grass-roots collective leadership has been able to free many mothers to return to work and enabled others who would otherwise have had to rely on welfare to take new jobs.

Many women in middle management and below, because of passivity or the fear of failure, or through uptight striving, remain fixed in old jobs, hesitating to venture. For them, no pep talks—only the reminder that they've no place to go but up, an energizing thought to perk up anyone's perspectives.

PART THREE

Soloing

12

Laying the Groundwork

In our survey of speech skills, we've progressed from the informality of conversation to more organized and purposeful forms: interviews, discussion groups, panel forums—and now, the solo public speech. A single thread ties these skills together: the two-way current of live communication—person-to-person or person-to-people. The basic concept doesn't change with an audience of one or of many, for *all speaking is public.*

Before proceeding with the practical "how-to's" of preparing and delivering a talk, there's an urgent question to consider: how to deglamorize all the hoopla over speechmaking. Especially, we must shake loose the "star" performance syndrome that handicaps many aspiring speakers.

The illusion of that lone figure, the speaker-performer, exhorting and inspiring thousands, lingers in the imagination. Even those who have never set foot on stage or platform will fantasize the recurrent nightmarish experiences of forgetting lines as they stand alone on a vast bare stage. Far removed from the illusion is the reality—talking with people out front about *some matter of mutual interest*—the essence of the good speech, anywhere, anytime.

To Speak or Not to Speak

Even with the nameless fears and fancies exposed and under control, women still have to deal with the actual fears of the stand-up speech. The spotlighted solo situation appears threatening; they shrink from expressing their opinions in public and from audience criticism, especially with men present; they tend to resist becoming involved and assuming responsibilities. These anxieties seesaw with universal wants—women want to be accepted, believed, admired, they want to triumph over timidity—and to move the minds and hearts of other women and of men.

Relax—public speaking is not a must. You can lead a satisfying, outgoing, and useful life without ever making that speech. Your experience in all likelihood has proven that speaking with small groups, the most important of all speech activities, gets things done—in committees, business conferences, study classes.

But if the bug has bitten—if you still long to surmount your nerves and mount a platform—then work up to the challenge. Begin with conversation—how well do you do in a living room? Women often insist that they do just fine with a small group at home, but that the moment they face those faces out front, facility takes flight. Despite this claim, one doubts their fluency even in the living room; what they seek is the comfort of a sheltered atmosphere. Who doesn't?

If at first you do succeed, try, try again. One day you're asked to chair a small meeting of a local committee on public housing and you function with scarcely a hitch; the next week comes the suggestion that you make a plug for the new community day-care center at the membership meeting of Planned Parenthood. You swallow the "Who, me?" and fill the assignment. Before you know it, you're on your feet, explaining and persuading. Now you've got your feet wet and the water, while cold, is bracing.

Should you take a public-speaking course? By all means, but first make a realistic estimate of what you expect to gain. Watch out for those "you-too-can-be" advertisements selling gold bricks of instant success.

Bona-fide courses, however, can be had in and out of colleges where the experience of delivering prescribed talks is all to the good. Traditional speech outlines, while boosting your logic on paper, may drown your talks in headings, subheadings, and roman numerals. Should you seek help with your voice in these courses, you're apt to find little except the increased volume you manage to produce when your turn comes to deliver a talk before the class.

Your topic and you. What *should* you, rather what do you *want* to speak about? No matter how well intentioned, no talk can mean much unless its subject moves you to express your thoughts and feelings. Problem-laden topics like the energy crisis, inflation, human rights, the divorce tangle, pollution, political corruption, concern us all. Of course, you will not be expected to deal with the totality of such subjects, any one of which could provide the basis for a full day's conference, complete with panels. Later we shall look into some less weighty matters with the purpose of entertaining an audience (a skillful business). For now, let us stay with the sort of problem you would hate to refuse to discuss if assigned.

Begin with a Story

You were probably read to as a child, your grandmother may have regaled you with many a never-to-be-forgotten tale, and you may have started with your own children on picture books (an excellent speech practice for them and for you). The narration form, regardless of content, has remained with you and now that you are tackling a talk, turn to storytelling as preparation.

Write out the first draft of your maiden speech as a story by answering the questions *who, where, when, what,* and *why,* and construct a plot line in logical sequence and suspenseful telling.

Let us suppose:

You are a consumer researcher. Your topic: "Up, Up and Away—The Soaring Prices." The story: This morning at the supermarket you ran into your friend Helen, and together you investigated several items and . . .

You are a volunteer social worker. Your topic: "Even If You Win, You Lose: A Case of Rape." The story: Alice Summers, who lives down the street (fictitious name and address) was assaulted by a rapist, and she went to court to press charges without corroboration and . . .

You are a single parent. Your topic: "Single Blessedness(?)." The story: This morning the children's schoolbus was late because of the weather and you missed the commuter train to your job and . . .

You are a lawyer. Your topic: "Mum's the Word or You're Fired?" The story: Rachel Smith, your client, has an employer who refuses illegally to hire married women, especially those with children and . . .

You were class president (Swarthmore, 1960). You are to speak at the class reunion on "Education for What?" The story: Your *cum laude* landed you a secretarial job at a large publishing house and . . .

Narration as a speech tool has many advantages: you can convert the whole of a story (if it fits) into your topic, or merely extract the nub of it to open your talk. Also, the tendency to cover nervousness with a stilted style of delivery is offset by the naturalness of recounting, rather than expounding. And with the telling on paper, you have warmed and humanized the approach to your topic, even if you eventually forgo the story itself.

The Speech as a Body

While we can dispense with some of the more complex methods of speech preparation that may hinder more than help, there are those enduring precepts, the eternal verities of speechcraft, that we cannot do without. From Plato in the fifth century B.C.: "Every speech ought to be put together like a living creature, with a body of its own, so as to be neither without head, nor without feet, but to have both a middle and extremities, described proportionately to each other and to the whole."

To develop a stable structure to lean on, *plan two-minute-by-the-clock talks on a single point;* these prepare you for the ten- to twenty-minute subjects with several points. The one-point workout gives you the bare bones of your topic, to which you later add the flesh. Following the classical image: the head is your introduction; the torso, your reasons, proofs, examples; the legs, your conclusion.

Choose a subject based on first-hand experience with the problem. You may decide on the forever-with-us fuel crisis. Your single-point topic: "A Program for Coping." To avoid bogging down on the introduction as many do by fussing with language, polishing a joke, and so on, *start with the body, not the head.*

First, *state the problem:* "We lived in an immobilized community—how did we get it rolling again?" Then list your proposals to ease the energy crunch: organize car pools; pay car-sitters to wait on gasoline lines for parents at work; charter the local bus service for evenings out and Saturday outings for children; press station wagons into service as an emergency volunteer taxi service; and so on. Your conclusion: *New energy* came with sharing responsibilities—proving that the good-neighbor policy is not just a slogan for yesterday.

Now *go back to your introduction* and fashion it to match *the conclusion* so that the whole body is in alignment. As an opener, variously known as the *grabber, awakener,* or (you should pardon the expression) *hooker,* you might select a historical reference or something in a light vein. As that old chestnut reminds us, "You tell 'em what you're gonna tell 'em—you tell 'em—you tell 'em what you told 'em."

Keeping the head-torso-legs plan in mind, try other two-minute one-pointers:

"Shortage or Rip-off?"—another aspect of the energy crisis (statistics are required).

"Who Will Take Grandma?"—is old age a fulfillment or disaster?

"How to Needle Your Senator"—the ratification of the Equal Rights Amendment is still on the agenda.

Whether you aim to inform or persuade or both, the same abbreviated "body form" will fortify your technique and see you through to the delivery of more ambitious talks on any subject.

". . . History is an everlasting possession . . ."
(Thucydides)

When you sit down to ponder a topic, do you feel as if you were starting from scratch? Well, you needn't; a visit to the public library will change your perspective. Novices seem oblivious to the resources underfoot, good managers as they may be in other matters. To find sustenance for your talk, take a chartered trip back into women's ancient history and from there onward, not neglecting, of course, your own personal history, the life experience that led to the growing involvement in your topic.

Hidden history. Women's role in the history books, almost all of them by and about men, has been sketchily reported, to say the least—which is exactly what historians did! Recently, prodigious efforts have been made to put women back in the annals of place and time. (For example, college courses in women's studies have increased from two in 1970 to seventy-two in 1973, from approximately 100 courses on sixty campuses to more than 2,000 courses on 500 campuses.) And the stream of literature devoted to ongoing female achievement continues unabated.

For background material in talks concerned with divorce, education, or politics, for example, here are some chronological clues, with Plato as keynoter:

> No calling in the life of the city belongs to woman as woman or to man as man; by nature the woman has a share in all practices, and so has the man. For a woman to hold the guardianship [hold office] she will not need special education. We will be dealing with the same nature in woman as in man and the same education will be required for both. (From Plato's *Republic*, translated by W. H. D. Rouse, New York, New American Library, 1956.)

Some Rapid Datelines

c. 700 B.C. When the antebellum culture flourished, the women of Sparta had considerable independence and authority.

c. 600 B.C. Athenian women were among the pupils of the great Greek philosophers.

A wife could obtain a divorce by judicial decision.

Plutarch (c. 100 A.D.) referred to these lenient divorce laws in Athens and in Rome as well. The grounds: the husband's age or poor health, or his extended absence on army duty at the front.

c. 500 B.C. Greek women of achievement were granted special awards of honorary citizenship.

A woman was chief magistrate of Priene.

Aristophanes wrote *Lysistrata*, his famous antiwar comedy about those indomitable ladies of Athens who waged and won their historic sexual rebellion.

c. 400 B.C. It was said of the Celtic women of pagan Gaul, "A whole troop of foreigners would not be able to withstand a single Gaul if he called his wife to his assistance, who is usually very strong, and with blue eyes." (From Myles Dillon and Nora Chadwick, *The Celtic Realms*, New York, New American Library, 1967.)

In Celtic law the husband and wife had equal rights under marriage contract.

The Dark Ages. "If [early] Christianity turned the clock of general progress back a thousand years, it turned back the clock two thousand years for women." (From Margaret Sanger, *Women and the New Race*, New York, Brentano's, 1920.)

"Cruelty and barbarity [rape] were more frequent . . . than in any civilization prior to our own." (From Will and Ariel Durant, *The History of Civilization*, Vol IV., "The Age of Faith," New York, Simon & Schuster, 1950.)

c. 600 A.D. St. Bridget was noted as a remarkable scholar.

c. 900 Lady Uallach was among Ireland's greatest poets.

c. 1300 "Philippa, as is usual with the brightest specimens of female excellence, was the friend of her own sex." (From Agnes Strickland, *Lives of the Queens of England*, Vol. II, Philadelphia, Lea & Blanchard, 1850.)

Philippa, as queen of England's Edward III, and patron of the arts, founded a college at Oxford, also the woolen and coal industries.

c. 1400 Women were licensed to practice law and medicine. Caecelia of Oxford was a famed physician of her time.

c. 1500 Sir Thomas More on women's education: "I cannot see why learning in like manner may not equally agree with both sexes."

Margaret Roper, who was the most brilliant of Sir Thomas's daughters, had this sympathetic note from her father deploring the doubt cast on her literary gifts: ". . . [Sweete Megg,] men [who] read your writings suspect you to have had help from some man . . ." (From Cresacre More, *The Life of Sir Thomas More* [1726] as quoted in Myra Reynolds, *The Learned Lady in England*, 1650–1760, Gloucester, Massachusetts, Peter Smith, 1964.)

To unearth more of this extraordinary story, follow through on your own by digging into chronicles, memoires, footnotes, and the like. As you progress through history, references to women become ever more frequent, providing a rich source for talks on many topics.

What's an original idea, anyway? A novel notion should have substance and use value, if possible, in the solution of a pending problem. Further, the idea should move from *what was* to *what is now* and on to *what is yet untried*. All originality comes down to this: something new growing out of the old, a sort of re-vision of the past. When the force of a newly begotten idea impels people into resolution and action, such an idea can properly be called *original.*

"Can a Woman Be President?" was the subject of a recent provocative speech by Marya Mannes, noted writer and speaker. She explored the probability and advantages of a woman's election in the next few decades to the most august position in the land. "Then— maybe," she declared to her rapt audience, "2000 will start the Century of the Human Being—the final fusion of the best qualities of both sexes in one person."

She concluded her talk with this *original* projection, adding, "Since I won't be around to hear it, I am taking the outrageous liberty of giving you the final phrases of her acceptance speech on the oc- casion of her nomination for President." Marya Mannes stirred her listeners with the vision of her message and the superb use of lan- guage and voice with which she delivered it. Read for yourself the "acceptance speech," at first silently and then aloud (p. 191).

The present, past, and future, then, can inform and inspire your talk—the recognition of today's pressing needs, the vivid recollection of the past and an intimation of the future—perhaps of an idea whose time will come.

We now turn to the *know-how*'s of preparing and delivering a talk. With these securely in hand, a stand-up speech, formerly for- midable, can become the familiar and comfortable experience of simply talking with people.

13

Creating the Speech

Getting It Together

President Woodrow Wilson was once asked how long he would prepare for a ten-minute talk. "Two weeks," he answered. "How long for an hour speech?" "One week," he said. "How long for a two-hour speech?" The President asserted, "I'm ready now."

Clearly, a short talk leaves no time for rambling; you must tighten the script in advance. A long-time rule directs us, however, to collect at least twice as much information as can be used.

Begin by making entries in a looseleaf notebook, always noting the source of any materials you've selected from books, magazine articles, newspapers. When dealing with a controversial matter, make doubly sure to document carefully all your quotes. To corral random thoughts on your topic, keep dropping slips into a manila folder; it's surprising how many lively bits can be accumulated in a week. But watch the temptation to prolong the treasure hunt and thus to delay the moment of committing your ideas to paper.

Perhaps you're a professional worker in the public-health field or a volunteer or just an aroused citizen. In any case, you're concerned about food—not with cooking it, nor with finding that inexpensive little restaurant, but about the sorry state of the National Market Basket (and your own supermarket cart).

Your notebook contains the hardware for your talk: clippings, several current exposés in hardcover, pamphlets (U.S. Government Printing Office), a transcript of an educational TV discussion, and more. Your manila folder holds the soft stuff: personal memos, some likely anecdotes, the week's encounter with tasteless tomatoes, fake whipped cream, beef-stretchers, and who knows what frozen goo.

After playing the game of the name for days, you've narrowed the choice of topic title to: "Your Food Is Killing You," "Our Food Scandals," or "Fake Food—or Who's Faking Now?"

Designing the Talk

Consider your aim: do you want to alert, inform, persuade, convince, inspire, or perhaps a little of each? You've already flexed your muscles on the one-point, two-minute talk, based on the classical head-torso-legs plan (p. 177). Proceed now with stretching this framework to encompass additional points and more detail.

Though your opening and closing remarks have been simmering for a while, start with outlining the main dish by combining the ingredients of *why, what* and *how*—your reasons, examples, and proposals. Where do you begin? In the kitchen.

Do you scribble your shopping list on the back of an envelope and then forget it? Of course not; you're organized and have been jotting down items all week long on the scratch pad magnetized to the refrigerator. Ready for shopping, you map a sensible sequence of the stops to make:

Supermarket—grocery items arranged in convenient order: dairy, meat, fresh vegetables, canned goods, etc.

Dry Cleaners—drop off woolen pants suit, is long skirt ready?

Shoemaker—Joe's shoes heeled, pick up my boots, scuff-covering polish.

Bakery—doz. dinner rolls, order Sue's birthday cake.

Post Office—mail spec. del. letter, buy roll of stamps, book of air mails.

Library—return books, reserve two (titles).

Pick up—Sue at Ellen's.

Because you know where you're headed, follow the same logical procedure with points linked to points and facts to facts. Carry over the design of your shopping list to a rational progression of the main points for your talk, and lined up under them, the items you intend to cover. Like this:

Working Title: *Is Your Food Killing You?*

Point 1. *The American Food Scandal.* Corporate giants contrive what we eat for higher profits . . . Danger and deficiencies in family diets threaten national health . . . We are being had (especially at these prices!).

Point 2. *The Hyper-risky American Diet.* Intake of dairy products, fresh vegetables, fruit *down* 25 per cent in 20 years; sugar-saturated snacks, soft drinks *up* 80 per cent . . . These teeth-rotters also breed serious diseases . . . Artificial colors, flavors, induce hyperactivity in children . . . Convenience foods save women time but cost plenty in money and poor nourishment.

Point 3. *The Yearly Corporate Harvest.* *$500 million* to drug companies for chemical additives . . . *$116 billion* to food and beverage industry for ever more synthetic and highly processed foods . . . *$2 billion* to snow us with ads in all media on nutritional humbug.

Point 4. *What Good Eating Is All About.* Restoring sound edibles to American tables: foodstuffs rated on vital content, well-balanced menus, and more groups organized to buy good food at wholesale.

Point 5. *The Big Must.* Government action essential to break the bind of corporate giants, ban dangerous additives, upgrade wheat products, expose consumer fraud . . . Women must bring about such urgent changes . . . Food, to become safe, must become part of politics.

A seasoned speaker could deliver that talk from the five-point synopsis. So could you, providing you had delivered it several times previously—*fully written out.* At this beginning stage, a spelled-out speech, securely in hand, will serve you best. Besides, many a platform veteran prefers a script to an outline, so you're in good company.

On the dining table, lay out your whole collection, the background material from the ringed notebook and all the personal slips from the folder. Handy are dictionary, thesaurus, and cassette. With the five-point synopsis as guide, set to work.

Since speaking and writing are two quite different modes of expression, avoid a literary approach. Use short (not abrupt) phrases and sentences, write *ear* copy, not *eye* copy. Simplicity does not mean dullness; ornate language can be very dull indeed. *Stodgy:* "I should like to inquire of those present—who will shoulder the financial responsibility?" *Straightforward:* "I ask—who'll foot the bill?" Your choice of words makes the difference in color and appeal.

The objective is to bring your topic and your listeners together, so tell it to them person to person. Let the language flow without stopping to edit, and leave lots of space between sentences for second thoughts. As your thoughts turn on, the basic five points hold together from first to last. Scatter throughout vivid statistics and quotes gleaned from your batch to liven the telling. Some samples:

> Children's TV program sells candy for breakfast with this commercial: "My super-sweet cereal [sic], chocolate-sweet for monster chocolate flavor."
>
> —*Washington Post*
>
> Many children, hyperactive as a result of food synthetics, are tranquillized in turn with Ritalin.
>
> —*Congressional Record*
>
> Baking corporations "refine" fourteen nutriments out of the flour and then put some of them back synthetically—the flour is then labeled "enriched."
>
> —*New York Review of Books*
>
> Our diets . . . are probably major causes of diabetes, coronary thrombosis, hypertension, and other "civilized" diseases.
>
> —Senate Select Committee on Nutrition and Human Needs

With the main body of your topic on paper, skip any alterations for the time being. Continue right on with the first draft to prepare your introduction.

Building a Bridge

To get smoothly in and out of a talk, your opening and closing should provide secure boundaries for you to cross. Important as the first friendly impression is, never pad the beginning; experiment with several approaches to make a shortened selection later. The wide choice of *awakeners* invites you to open with a leading question or a punchy statement, a personal story or converted old joke, a notable quote or a wise saying.

It would seem that the subject of food has stayed with you every working and idle moment as fresh notions for your talk kept popping into your head. Though your talk is serious, you needn't be glum, and your firsthand references and personal anecdotes make the warmest way to greet an audience. If something amusing or significant of your own doesn't strike you as quite right for an opener, head for the library to find speech books with jokes, anecdotes, aphorisms listed according to subject. Look over those indexed under Food, and if the material often has a dated ring, never mind. When updated and adapted to the purpose at hand, humorous material will sound fresh.

The next important step. *Find a link between the anecdote and your topic.* Try this for an opener (revised and personalized): My mother used to serve what she called her *enthusiastic stew:* she put everything she had into it! Suggest that your talk is like an *enthusiastic stew.* The more involved you became with the subject of food frauds, the more of yourself you put into it. Now you want to share your angry stew; then go right into your first point, the American food scandal. Reworking a joke and finding the angle, once you get the hang of it, is more fun than work.

Or perhaps you prefer to open with a couple of *did-you-know-that*'s. Try these attention-getters:

Did you know that in 1939 the American symbol, the hot dog, contained 19 per cent protein and 19 per cent fat; in *1946*—15 per cent protein and 14 per cent fat; and by *1969*—11 per cent protein and 30 per cent fat? Imagine the ratio *today.*

Did you know that pizza, when frozen, is hyped up by injections of artificial color and flavoring to *look rich* in tomato sauce?

From this vantage point, you're practically into your topic.

The Windup

Handle the finish with finesse; it conveys the last impressions the audience takes away. You can't expect people to remember what you said only once—the significant ideas always bear careful repetition. And you can't just dish out a quick summary and be gone. Decide what you want the listener to remember and repeat the nub of your five points (rephrased). Refrain from enumerating. "I have made five points..." will keep them counting instead of concentrating on content. After retelling what you told, wind up with something memorable, just as in the opener, the provocative reference or anecdote contributed to a smooth take-off.

Keep pouring out the prose as the end approaches; it's still not time for a polish job. The writing has clarified your theme, what an actress would term the *spine* of a scene that supports all the ideas and holds the scene together.

Uncovering the food story, you discover your own motivation and "We must *do* something" begins pulsing through your thinking. True, your talk is factual, statistical, informative, but underneath, a current of urgency carries you along.

Though the curtain is about to ring down, don't *let* down until you've formed the shape of the finale—perhaps the right quote, or a personal bit you've saved for last, or a rousing plea for increased consumer education, for trained volunteers to track down complaints, for a corps of lobbyists to put muscle behind a new Federal Food Protection Bill.

Paring It Down

The question of length did not restrict the stream of consciousness now confided to paper—everything flowed together, what you already knew about the subject along with what you learned from reading. Though you rambled a little on your way, the five-point guideposts (p. 183) held you to the main road. Comes the moment to remember the ten-minute limit on your talk; and here's a practical procedure to reduce the extended first draft to the alloted time.

1. *Read it all aloud.* Attach the beginning and end to the middle of your food story: if you're comfortable with the cassette as a home study companion, a recording of the rough version will benefit, not throw, you. Otherwise, better wait for the cut version. Meanwhile, trust your ear to catch the warm ring of words as you tell it aloud the way you wrote it—person to person.

2. *Begin to edit.* Blue-pencil the words that looked good in writing and sound stuffy as you speak them. Substitute more informal language to convey the sense of immediacy. Pruning can be painful, but be severe with yourself. Do you hate to discard such personal anecdotes as the references to that trick diet on which you gained weight and went broke, or the sandwich of wholesome dark bread your

kids rejected because other schoolchildren always brought that nice soft white packaged stuff? Take heart; the attractive material you reluctantly forgo could contribute nicely to the question and answer period.

3. *Cut and paste.* Materials: scissors, construction paper, rubber cement (practical for peeling off and rearranging items). First snip from your pages the telling sentences that appear most likely to belong together. Once pasted on heavier paper, you can judge how well they sound when joined. Keep redesigning the talk in this fashion until satisfied with the continuity, based on the five original headings. Leave wide margins on the new page for inserting personal reminders and plenty of space between sentences or groups of sentences.

4. *Have the paste-up copied.* Photostating machines are readily available (at libraries, etc.). The seams and smears on the reassembled, reduced version won't show up when copied. The pages will look sharp, coherent, and ready for practice and timing (to be strictly gauged in advance).

5. *Underscore the salient points* in red and lesser points in green, as you read through the revised script.

6. *Standing up to your speech.* Practice on your feet; it's a waste of time mumbling while lounging in a chair. Give your voice full play; if you expect to have a mike later, then take the voice down as required. The feedback of bigger sound is reassuring. This time turn on the cassette—by now self-listening has grown more objective. Whatever discomfort still persists is a small price to pay for the many advantages.

Place a table in front of a long mirror, resting the script on top of some large volume so you can read without bending over. Keep in sight an open-faced, inexpensive timepiece—those tiny wrist models are useless. Pacing yourself, figure on talking nine, not ten, minutes (a safe if small margin). Rehearse the material in three-minute intervals, breaking off at logical points.

To release tenseness, sit with your feet up; or stretch out on the floor; or do some simple head rolls and breathe rhythmically (the Good Breath, p. 28). Then back on your feet to rehearse for three minutes more followed by the brief rest period. In this manner, you keep to a comfortable, relaxed pace while reading and avert the tendency to speed up—a common failing.

Don't get lost in the mirror; stand off from it and see yourself in a generalized way, visualizing how you look from a distance. Consult the mirror frequently to test your ability to *look at the audience.* Arrange, if possible, a live rehearsal before a friend or a group—even better, a speech workshop.

Preparing to Deliver

There are three ways to deliver a speech: you can give it from memory; you can speak it from an outline; or you can read it to the audience.

1. The *memorized* speech that depends on automatic recall is fraught with danger unless you're a gifted actress who can give the illusion of performing the whole of it for the first time. Memorizing turns the concentration inward instead of out and that glazed look in your eye comes from trying to recall that clever phrase at the bottom of page three. Like the child who, reciting a poem, forgets and has to start all over again from the beginning, should you lose the train of thought and want to get back on track, you might be forced to repeat the whole paragraph!

2. The *outline* approach is a method touted by most authorities and ducked by most beginners. For experienced speakers, the outline has obvious benefits: *stability* and tight structure (usually on cards) and *flexibility* in a conversational style of delivery.

For many women, however, these advantages are cold comfort, even when the opening and closing are written out and memorized (also recommended). They may take off smoothly enough and then stumble through the terse listing of ideas abbreviated on cards. Understandably, many aspiring if unskilled women have been turned off by what seems like an extra burden. They tend to fumble the cards nervously or to hold them tensely lest one drop to the platform (it generally does).

There is no earthly reason to force yourself to accept this means of giving a talk or to feel defeated if you don't—as if the form rather than the spirit were paramount.

Some suggestions for the accomplished card-handler: make sure the material is uncluttered and well spaced, and readable at arm's length. The cards, measuring at least 4½ x 6 inches and conspicuously numbered, should have key points underlined in color. Since lecterns rarely accommodate the needs of speakers, it is advisable to place the cards on books or handbag at eye level, propped against an improvised support.

The woman speaking is the *medium* of communication, *not* the method. Wait until you know the material like the back of your hand; then, if it adds security, opt for an outline; otherwise forget it, and *read your talk.*

3. *Reading a speech* has, as a technique, a bad reputation with speech teachers, nonspeakers, and listeners, who far too often have been bored by the monotony of droning voices dropping off at the end of every sentence. Also, before a word is uttered, an obvious sheaf of papers will raise a paper curtain between talker and hearer. Of course, learning how to read aloud *effectively* makes all the difference, and furnishes a security blanket no other form of delivery can match.

Of the three, this method demands the most preparation and generally receives the least: therein lies the pitfall. Unless you invest time in developing facility as a reader, the result can indeed be deadly dull. With an attentive ear for the live patterns of good conversation—the flow of phrases and the pauses between them—anyone can, with practice, transfer a living-room skill to the somewhat larger than life effect from the platform.

Remember, reading a talk with communicative effect by seeming not to read is an *acquired skill.* Meanwhile, if there's a talk coming up, don't hold off, read it aloud the best you can. Experience will teach you plenty as you gradually acquire this skill.

The How-to's

Speaking off the page. If you stay with the routine of scanning several words ahead, then look up and speak the words clearly in succession, your eye will develop the ability to take in more and more words, a whole phrase or sentence. It's something like the technique for developing speed reading (silent), except that speed is not your goal. TV newscasters and others demonstrate the skill of appearing *not to read,* when actually they do read from cue cards off screen to give the impression of speaking right *at* you.

Coordinating the action. How often should you deliver a line off the page? At most, a third of your total time. Eventually, the meaning will dictate the length of the phrase you choose to say directly to the audience. Hold the phrase in your mind, resisting the impulse to spill it all at once—you *know* what you're going to say.

An example: During your talk on food and with these lines already in your head, deliver them conversationally, to ask, "Do you feed your children candy for breakfast?" *Wait,* then add, "You *do* when they eat"—now hold for suspense—*"sugar-coated cereal!"* The eye contact helps you to measure the length of pauses. Overcome what is called in speech parlance "the fear of silence," displayed by most novices; the mark of the assured speaker is the ability to *hold the pause.*

Important: Don't speak on your way up from the page; only when you have met your listeners' eyes should you deliver the line. Otherwise you lose the lifelike patterns of talk. Pace your reading, both on *and* off the page, with this inherent rhythm of talking *with* people.

Practicing, practicing. As you experiment at home with this lively way of making a talk, eye muscles *and* feelings of security grow stronger. Rereading aloud, you absorb much of the language; the content grows on you. Freed from the page, spoken lines take on new dimension—what an actress would call a "truthful reading."

Some devices. You may prefer easier-to-read capital letters for the text; or use a Speech Writer typewriter, with extra large, type size 29 (you won't need glasses). Enclose your pages in an attractive folder—no one will ever suspect how few or how many you have. Doing your stint in public is always tough the first couple of times, no matter what method you employ. Reading aloud with eye rapport lends you the best support when you need it the most.

The ultimate speech. The three methods of delivery, when combined, are tools of skilled speechcraft in the hands of an expert. She can create an effect of extemporaneous conversation from a few spare notes or from a memorized essay or story ("I think it goes like this . . ."); and then at the conclusion, her eyes meeting eyes out front, she will read a poem aloud in a way to lift the spirit.

As you progress in your delivery, whichever form works best for you, take it for your own to be used again and again. It's like making a sandwich, you can change the filling but the form remains the same.

While laying the groundwork for speechmaking, let us take time out for some reading aloud. Consider this practice period a polish job (not an overhaul) to inject added vigor to voice, clarity to words, and facility to that coming talk. *The aim:* to carry over into your platform delivery the expressive skills, first tested in rehearsal with some stimulating prose. Repetitious rereading of your talk can bring diminishing returns; you'll find it regenerating to work out on material other than your own.

The first selection comes from the speech by Marya Mannes entitled "Can a Woman Be President?" The excerpt for study is part of a woman's acceptance speech on the occasion of her nomination circa 1998 as President of the United States (as envisioned by Ms. Mannes).

Your approach to the material will, of course, affect the delivery. Avoid feeling overawed by the content; perform the lines with simplicity and directness despite the vast imagined audience listening in—on TV, via satellite, or from the moon! Overcome any tendency to rush or to slur; first, last, and always, speak as distinctly as possible.

Designs for clarity in reading aloud. The sentences have been grouped progressively and numbered; each group, from 1 to 6, exemplifies an expressive technique with special, easy-to-follow markings. As you proceed, refer to the following pages for the instructions with corresponding numbers (1 to 6).

(1) The HONor beSTOWed on me toNIGHT is enTIREly your HONor: the HONor to VOTE for a HUman BEing and NOT a poLITical COMpromise.

(2) Yours is the first party ... to realize that a human being— whether biological man or biological woman—is composed of the moral, intellectual, and spiritual attributes of both sexes ...

(3) ... war is the worst pestilence on earth, and the worst / solution. // The only conceivable reason for combat—more / deadly in each decade of advanced technology—is the rape by violence / of our

own country—this land / these United States. There is no other / justification for killing. //

(4) And I promise you now that—should I become President—

no Pentagon, no cabinet, no Congress, no Chief of Staff, will

force me into the act of war for any other reason than self-defense.

(5) And if by chance there should occur a peaceful invasion of our

country by little blue men from another planet—more intelligent than

ours—then we should welcome them—rather than massacre them. We

could use their help!

(6) Let us pledge each other, above all else, that we are committed to life. A life in which people can grow and learn and achieve and create in peace and freedom. A life in which we can save this country—this beautiful land of ours—from the forces of greed and neglect and rapacity which even now threaten it.

For this we *must* fight. I love you. Dear friends—dear Americans—good night!

Now to work. Begin with the basics. Wake up your voice with ten minutes of setting-up drills, choosing the ones that you've found most beneficial in Chapter 2. Why not try humming, the simplest tuning up of all, and/or "say and sing," that enjoyable and remedial routine?

We've worked with all these techniques before and you are reworking them here in a progression to build the communicative content of your reading delivery and, from there, into your platform performance.

Now match the instructions to the excerpt as the numbers direct (1 through 6).

(1) *The built-in beat.* Accent the capitalized word segments and tone down all others. Do you feel the inherent rhythms that convey

meaning in our language? English demands contrasts between *strong* and *weak* word types and syllables *within* words. Don't, however, hit at the sounds, or the words will jump at the listener; rather, *lean* tonally on the stressed elements.

(2) *Think link.* Continue to stress and unstress accurately, and at the same time follow smoothly the marked interconnected line. Observe how, taken together, the built-in beat and linked words fall *sensibly* and *pleasantly* on listening ears. (This is what your talk should accomplish.)

(3) *The versatile pause.* Note the slash mark (/) to indicate a short pause, and the double slash (//) a longer pause. Sometimes the suggested slashes correspond with the punctuation, and other times not; the meaning takes you to a creative pause, which is not necessarily determined by a comma. These fragments of silence should act:

—as a breather (literally) and a resting point for you *and* the audience;

—as an attention-holder with a steady glance;

—as emphasis *before* or, at times, *after* a word;

—as signals for change in the three "variables" that add variety (speed, pitch, and volume) to your delivery—speaking *faster or slower, higher or lower, louder or softer.*

Do the indicated pauses correspond with those you might choose? If not, make your own, and forbear to hurry past; if necessary, *count to three* before you go on. Work to perfect these pauses that often speak louder than words. As you follow the slashes, can you relate them to your talk?

(4) *Don't play that rundown melody.* To offset the monotonous effect and loss of meaning from dropping energy toward the ends of phrases, follow the gradual increase of volume as marked by the crescendo signs (⊏⎯⎯⎯⎯). Also check with the "and" remedy, page 102. Develop adeptness at lifting all sagging lines, especially the often indispensable *final* words; and watch your delivery spark as a result.

(5) *Emphasis: the choice is yours.* Apart from the natural stresses of the language itself, we emphasize words as their meaning strikes us. Follow the suggested underlining: a single line to point up a word and a double one for extra emphasis. Interpret the underscoring to heighten and dramatize the excerpt.

(6) The *built-in beat* plus the *linking action* plus the *versatile pause* plus *sustaining the tonal line,* plus your own *emphasis,* add up to a dynamic totality. Combine all the practiced techniques in this sixth and final section, performing chosen phrases in your best *off-the-page style.*

Playback and checkup. Did you use your cassette consistently during the progressive integration of skills into your reading? You will want your ear attuned to the effect of what you gained in practice.

The "acceptance speech" conceived by Ms. Mannes will serve as a model for two more intermissions coming up. These will also feature prose selections to instruct and enrich your reading. Our objective remains the same: to transfer the tested results to the words you will speak face to face with a live audience. Speech coordinations, once firmly established, will persist, and your body will "remember."

14

The Audience, the Chair, and the Speaker

Who's Out Front?

Does the audience loom up like some hydra-headed monster, teeth bared? You're running a slight fever, otherwise you'd recognize them as people with whom you've simply changed places for the time being.

Actually, audiences are nicer than people, easier to talk to. They won't talk back or challenge you at every turn, at least not until the question period, and by then you've had your say. Besides, there's the nice attentive hush before you start. Can you count on that in a living room or in the office lounge?

You begin to feel that if you don't look an audience in the eye, it's impolite. Before beginning the talk, scan the room and notice that a listener can show nervousness, too—a pair of eyes will go down when meeting yours. If toward the end all eyes remain steadily upon you, you've made it!

Take the audience into your confidence and their body attitudes, murmurs, and laughter will reply. If sometimes the right word doesn't come, why not just wonder out loud what it might be, "What *is* a children's doctor called? The word simply escapes me." And someone will surely call out, "Pediatrician!" Smile and bow, "Thank you very much!" and the audience will laugh and like you for being fallible and frank.

Obviously your talk should fit the people for whom you designed it. While many topics cut across considerations of age, sex, education, we can still make some educated guesses as to who would spark to what subject.

Use this eight-point checklist of questions to help you tailor your talk to your listeners:

1. *"What's the size of the house?"* an actress will query before making her entrance. Advance knowledge of the size of an audience concerns all performers on stage or platform. A small gathering calls for an informal, "between-us" approach; for five hundred ticket-buyers, you must widen the angle of the subject, change or drop some "in" references or jokes, and make adjustments in voice and manner of delivery.

2. *What's the age range?* A reference to World War II makes acute sense to an older group; to a group under thirty-five, it's ancient history. They would respond to the title "The Vietnam Veteran Blues," while "Your Personal Population Control" might leave listeners over fifty somewhat cool. A title like "Health Care: More —Better—Cheaper" would bring out the mature crowd and their daughters and sons of child-rearing age might come along, too.

3. *Are they a female, male, or mixed audience?* Women are responding to formerly "masculine" issues (prison reform, capital punishment, corruption in government), and men are increasingly drawn to what were principally "feminine" concerns (the family, child care, education). Titles like "Should Fathers Have Custody?" and "Whatever Became of Sin?" would rouse both sexes. While some women would leave the subject "Is God a Woman?" strictly alone, the attendance at that meeting would probably be an enthusiastic, all-female crowd.

4. *What prejudices are they prone to?* The blurring of such terms as *conservative, liberal, radical,* should prompt us to proceed with caution in applying them to audiences. Again, we can hazard some opinion concerning the reception certain topics would encounter. Controversial matters like capital punishment, sex before marriage, legalized abortion, may arouse hostility, even heckling. If you're invited or volunteer to give a talk before a conservative church group on "The Right to Bear or Not to," how should you proceed?

Begin by admitting quietly that you're aware that most women present are probably against legalized abortion, then request their tolerance and open-mindedness in hearing your side. (Here quote from an unimpeachable source.) Explore all the common ground you have as women and, without theatrics, let history and statistics dramatize your presentation.

Some speakers dealing with controversial matters suggest that both a neutral chairperson and meeting ground be agreed upon by both sides. Clearly, this is no job for a beginner; to venture into such troubled waters at all requires experience and deep commitment.

5. *Is yours a group with a special community of interest?* After you find out, there's some homework ahead in background research on the sponsoring group or organization. The more familiar you sound about the members' special interests, the warmer will be your reception.

Some of the established and more recent women's professional groups represent: doctors, lawyers, real-estate agents, film makers, TV reporters, engineers, architects, sportswomen. Immerse yourself in relevant shop talk of the profession and make the most of specific references in your talk. You have come perhaps to speak in behalf of a woman's candidacy for lieutenant governor, or the plight of women prisoners, or other matters of particular concern to this audience.

6. *What will they laugh at?* You can tell an X-rated joke to a younger group and reserve a subtler anecdote for a mature one.

7. *How informed are they?* Whether your listeners are not, somewhat, or well informed on the topic makes a difference in your choice of materials and language, though the express purpose of your talk would remain the same.

8. *What's their opinion of you?* Presumably the topic appeals to those gathered, yet they know little or nothing about you. Tell them yourself, especially why *you* are standing up there—"I am a teacher ... mother ... divorcee ... (or all three), and I am concerned about ..." Tell them how the subject has turned you on and, hopefully, may turn them on, too.

Question, Anyone?

A good speaker regards the audience as a partner—the working, not the silent kind—who participates thoughtfully throughout a talk, lecture, or meeting. The test of the partnership's success comes at the question-and-answer period, when the audience plays its part with the respect implicit in democratic practice. If hands go up at the conclusion, we know that the speaker has scored, and both partners can share the rewards of free discussion.

Often it may take a little coaxing to get things started. The enterprising host of the occasion, otherwise known as The Chair, has already set the stage for a keen but amiable interchange between those assembled and their mutual guest. She has:

—*consulted* with the speaker as to what points to elicit in the questions, especially those likely to be curtailed by the time limit;

—*coopted* a couple of poised members to initiate, if necessary, planted queries from the floor (written out in advance);

—*reserved* some questions for herself if all else fails, suggesting perhaps, "We [never "I"] have probably all wondered if . . ."

The speaker and the chair work as a team to:

—*make sure* that everyone hears the question;

—*repeat* an indistinct question, directing it out front;

—*rephrase* an awkward question if necessary;

—*encourage* every participant to speak up;

—*discard* (politely) a question off the point.

A seasoned speaker:

—*appreciates* this person-to-people opportunity of give and take;

—*projects* a feeling of personal warmth, but carefully avoids becoming "personal";

—*looks directly* at the questioner, then her eyes gather in other listeners to include them in her answer;

—*answers concisely,* without any sense of rush;

—*stays on the point,* resisting all temptation to wander;

—*fields difficult questions* with skill;

—*admits not knowing "all the answers"* ("Would anyone like to tackle that one?");

—*smiles,* never losing her cool, even if provoked;

—*handles a heckler* with tongue-in-cheek restraint;

—*proposes,* if feasible, *an informal rap session* for those who want to stay on after the meeting.

The questioner. Gertrude Stein, when asked at the very close of her life, "What is the answer?" is said to have replied, "What is the *question?"* Apparently, there is no final answer, only new questions.

As an individual and a member of the audience, thus far a silent partner in the discussion, you decide perhaps uncertainly to ask a question. How to begin? Put your idea on paper—the back of the program. Try to make your question concrete, relevant to the subject, and brief.

And no matter how personal your approach, the question should reflect the interest of others. Surely what you seek to know embraces a wider concern than your own. Women need to learn how to proceed from the particular to the general, to see themselves in thought and action in a larger social context. Most important of all, don't be hemmed in by doubts—*ask!*

If you're a skilled hand at posing questions (thereby raising the level of discussion), others will follow your lead. As the topic involves more and more people and comment, those on the floor and those on the platform will seem to merge and reason together in search of answers.

Who's in the Chair?

Chairman? Madame Chair*man?* (Ridiculous!) Hostess? Toastmistress? (Outrageous!) *Chairperson* seems to be in, but why not simply address her by name? All titles aside, any woman who has once been captain of a softball team, a den mother, cheerleader, or camp counselor can preside over a meeting.

The ideal Chair might embody some of these qualities:

1. *She's a coordinator,* in control without dominating, a firm but flexible timekeeper who sees that all runs smoothly: checks the heat, light, table, lectern, mike (if any), and seating arrangements; she stations a lookout at the back of the hall to test acoustics. She has a prepared, orderly agenda with relaxed rules of procedure that *work* and don't confuse.

2. *She works on herself,* paying diligent attention to voice and speech, posture and facial expression, knowing that when she opens her mouth to call the members to order, she sets the tone for the whole meeting. An inveterate note-taker, she remembers names by jotting them down. Always in the public eye, she's the model of a good listener (you'll never catch her napping). The saving grace of

humor lends her a light touch, essential to her job (when serious, women tend to look grim).

3. *She's a self-editor,* avoiding trite openers—especially that lame one, "Tonight's speaker needs no introduction," and those superadjectives: "brilliant," "scintillating," "witty," "internationally famous" (almost no one can measure up to such salutations!). Sensitive to her role, she passes the ball to others less proficient than she, even when time presses.

4. *She knows where her head is at,* and never slumps at the conclusion with a weary "That's all, folks." Her goal is to motivate: she urges self-expression to break through isolation by speaking out. While not a paragon (though it may seem so), our woman in the chair can grow with this job into a leader.

Rules of Order

To conduct a meeting of an organization obliges the presiding person to have a working knowledge of *parliamentary procedure.* This weighty term sometimes intimidates women, especially those who hang back at meetings, hesitating to speak up. Relaxed rules for efficient functioning evolve best in the process of members acting in concert. Which existing rules—how many, if any—apply to your affiliations? What are the more flexible and democratic guides for leader and member?

After a century of reprints and revisions, the prestige of *Robert's Rules of Order* remains intact, though, like the motel bedside Bible, the work itself is seldom thumbed. While his principles endure, his complicated rituals of parliamentary procedure no longer suit the tenor and tempo of our times.

As members of associations we continue to enjoy four basic rights—of the majority to prevail, of the minority to be heard, of all members to be equal, and to have the right of free discussion. In addition, we depend on ground rules to ensure these rights against violation and to facilitate the business of meetings. We require as well a handy, updated manual of procedure to aid and not to burden our efforts at self-government.

Legalistic jargon, in an autocratic leader's grasp, becomes, by thwarting the will of the majority, a potent weapon for control. Similarly, an obstructionist clique can maneuver to subvert the decisions of the membership.

At the other extreme, a loosely permissive leadership and atmosphere, by ignoring commonsense rules, will turn meetings into chaos. The result: those in attendance lose patience and interest, and the meeting goes nowhere.

Do you belong to an established women's group which operates exclusively and smoothly at the top, while the body of members remains silently inactive? *After* the meeting, invariably, loosened tongues speak with the freedom absent in the formal session. Or perhaps you've joined a new women's club where a typical meeting sounds like a gabfest of personal chatter and non sequiturs, and the actual business is left to small committees of women willing to do the work.

What's needed is agreed-upon regulation—neither stringent nor lax. *Most important:* enjoy self-education in *"Roberta's* Rules of Order," tailored to fit a membership jealous of its rights and eager to participate. Try these:

Roberta's Rules of Order

—*Do without procedure* if teamwork operates successfully without it.

—*Submit the agenda* to a vote of those present; a predetermined agenda often shuts off the impetus to participate.

—*Put aside reading of the minutes;* instead, mail them in advance of the next meeting.

—*Take care of new business before the old*—for better results and more prompt attendance.

—*Decide a question by consensus* rather than by voting; "taking the sense of the meeting" is a time-honored procedure. But *do vote* as a means to expedite pressing problems.

—*Have at the ready a small package of essential motions* protecting the rights of members and assuring spontaneous, fruitful operation (see bibliography for these basic and simple motions).

—*Dispense with the old custom of seconding a motion*—to speed agendas and encourage the making of motions (remember: only one at a time).

—*Consider all meetings legal* without a quorum present. Make only "must" decisions by quorum, previously set at a reasonable percentage of the membership.

Saying a Few Words

You've been tagged to *say a few words,* a euphemism for a short prepared talk to be presented at a formal dinner for a colleague about to retire, the christening celebration of your best friend's firstborn, your boss's birthday party for two hundred at the Ritz, the yearly ball of the Women's Lawn Tennis Association, a ceremony to accept the Woman of the Year Award in your hometown, population 5,000. Do you begin at once to agonize, imagining yourself on a dais, making a complete ass of yourself?

An entertaining talk doesn't mean a mishmash of funny stories, nor a deadpan delivery of gags like a stand-up comic. The most appealing stories nearly always spring from personal experience, *fitted to the occasion;* audiences love amusing anecdotes at your expense.

When you catch the sound of responsive laughter, remember not to talk through it or to laugh yourself unless the joke really is on you. Remind family and friends to restrain their overcompensating reactions, lest they be the only ones to laugh. Pretend to lose yourself in narration, looking over the heads as if trying to recollect some event. Actually, you've been rehearsing for a week; wasn't it Mark Twain who said that it took him three weeks to prepare an *impromptu* speech?

When chairing a meeting, *introducing a speaker* would be part of your function, or you may be asked to present some notable person at a formal occasion. Play a graceful and modest role in setting the stage for the star. Shunning the clichés—"It gives me great pleasure to . . ." or "I have the honor . . ."—substitute what comes naturally—"How pleased [or delighted, or proud] I am to introduce . . . [or to perform this assignment]."

Follow the old rules that still work:

—Stand with ease, phrase smoothly, put your best voice forward;

—Take no more than two minutes for this prologue (practiced and timed in advance);

—Give the title of the speech and remark on the audience's interest in the subject (don't be glib lest you misinform them);

—Choose selectively from biographical detail and highlight major achievements. Pass up extravagant praise, but point up the speaker's unusual fitness for making the talk;

—Pronounce her or his name accurately, smile, wait for an answering nod, and step out of the limelight.

There are scores of standard routines, each one filling a purpose, and all of them good speech practice: the bread-and-butter announcements, reports, introductions, community soliciting of funds, and speeches for nominations, presentations, and tributes. Though most of these conventions have lost old-time fustian trappings, they still function in today's settings. In this nation of award-givers and prize-winners, of ceremonies and celebrations, people find themselves frequently called upon to "say a few [hopefully well-chosen and well-spoken] words."

Grasp each opportunity to speak solo in public; never mistakenly consider any task so trifling as not to require preparation; remember that the appeal such public communication offers must still depend on the speaker's ability to be heard and understood. While these minor (often mini-) talks may not make you an orator, they are civilized tools that smooth the demands of custom and efficient function in a hundred and one ways.

Time again for reading-aloud practice. The paragraphs here numbered 1 through 6 correspond with those on pp. 192–94, which list a progression of techniques to aid your study. Note that the excerpt from Lillian Hellman's book *Pentimento* is not marked. Insert your own markings: (1) *stress patterns,* (2) *linking,* (3) *pauses,* (4) *crescendo increase* of volume, (5) *underlined words for emphasis,* and (6) pulling them all together for a *grand total.*

This excerpt should be spoken with quiet intimacy—as if you yourself were reminiscing about the past, perhaps in a long anecdote—the personal quality makes very good listening in a stand-up speech.

From the Foreword to the book:

(1) Old paint on canvas, as it ages, sometimes becomes transparent. When that happens it is possible, in some pictures, to see the original lines: a tree will show through a woman's dress, a child makes way for a dog, a large boat is no longer on an open sea. That is called *pentimento* because the painter "repented," changed his mind.

(2) Perhaps it would be as well to say that the old conception, replaced by a later choice, is a way of seeing and then seeing again. That is all I mean about the people in this book. The paint has aged now and I wanted to see what was there for me once, what is there for me now.

Here, Lillian Hellman reminisces about her second play, *Days to Come:*

(3) . . . The failure of a second work is, I think, more damaging to a writer than failure will ever be again. It is then that the success of the first work seems an accident and, if the fears you had as you wrote it were dissipated by the praise, now you remember that the praise did not always come from the best minds and even when it did it could have been that they were not telling the truth or that you had played good tricks.

(4) And you are probably too young, too young at writing, to have found out that you really only care what a few people think; only

they, with the change in names that time brings about, will stand behind your chair for good or bad, forever.

(5) But failure in the theatre is more public, more brilliant, more unreal than in any other field. The praise is usually out of bounds: the photographs, interviews, "appearances," party invitations are so swift and dazzling that you go into the second work with confidence you will never have again if you had any sense.

(6) . . . It is hard for me to believe these many years later in the guilt I felt for the failure of *Days to Come;* the threads of those threads have lasted to this day. Guilt is often an excuse for not thinking and maybe that's what happened to me. In any case, it was to be two years before I could write another play, *The Little Foxes,* and when I did get to it I was so scared that I wrote it nine times.

Check up and follow through. Did you enjoy the *Pentimento* excerpt while working on it? Did the cassette confirm your guess that the planned practice enhanced your reading? So far, so good. From now on, what you gained from your reading-aloud experience should dovetail with your delivery in giving a talk.

15

Delivery

The term "delivery," with its many-layered meaning, is especially expressive for women. A composite definition says why: giving birth, a "blessed event," a creative act, a handing over, any giving forth, a rescue, liberation, release, and—*the manner of style of uttering a speech!*

Nervous?

The soothing syrup served up in most speech books rarely makes one feel any better. We are told that *fear* comes from *adrenaline* rushing to your glands and stirring you up, so that you can give your best; or that, if you have nervous tension, how lucky you are! Without it you'd be in bad shape—just a clod, really, and inevitably a boring, smug speaker. And if you wonder who's afraid, the answer is everybody! The big names testify that what makes a pro is the *practice* of being afraid.

Nervousness, of varied origin, is real enough. It is often created by the gap between reality and fantasy—a sort of "colosseum complex." The antidote: instead of imagining the situation in grandiose terms, see the scene *as it is*. As you look out front, and the faces come into focus, note their humanness and friendliness. Although you refuse to believe it, also be assured that while your heart may hammer and your knees feel odd, signs of the jitters seldom show.

The best pacifier, now and always, is your rehearsed script on the lectern before you and the opening and closing lines in your head. Standing feet apart, one foot slightly ahead of the other (feet *feeling*

206

the floor), with shoulders released, your stance reassures you and the audience. Your body doesn't have that unyielding, squared-away look that some women affect. First you thank the chairperson *by name* for the pleasant introduction. *Now you're talking!*

Platform Pointers

Make a selection from this collection—yours to *work toward.*

1. *At ease.* Do you manage to appear poised at a social gathering or public function? Then consider this "speaking in public" no exception. How do you begin?

2. *Establish rapport.* Strike an informal note early with such questions as: "Anybody need to put a dime in the meter before we begin?" "Is it too hot? Shall we turn the heat down?" "Since one of our guests is late, shall we wait a few more minutes?" "Can you hear me back there?" "I see some empty rows at the front. Why don't you all move up closer?"

Always think of the audience ahead of yourself; turn the spotlight outward toward them.

3. *Smile the while.* Banish the notion that you must have a serious mien to be taken seriously. But don't overreact and grin your way through the talk; relax facial expression, smile with eyes letting your warmth come through.

4. *Shifting gears.* Stay loose by shifting your position periodically—not with a large movement when a slight one will do; begin with the feet to permit your body to follow suit.

You Amplified

5. *The mike.* Stand back about eight inches, closer if your voice doesn't carry well; but don't move in so cozily close that you feel tempted to croon. Speak *toward* the mike, *not into it.* You should dominate the instrument, not vice versa; don't keep staring at it, look beyond at the audience.

Amplification exaggerates all sound: curtail noisy breathing and watch popping consonants like /p/, /t/, and /k/. Move within the possible limits of lectern and mike. Did you remember to test the amplification before you started?

Without a mike, you'll have to amplify your own voice, turning up the volume without straining.

Our Physical Dialogue

6. *What does your body say?* Important moments in body language: your entrance and exit. So don't march on like a martinette, nor slink in like the Invisible Woman. Walk with easy, released posture—both coming and going—well rehearsed in advance.

Rest your fingers on the lectern or table. *Do* gesture by all means. Make a point of using hand and arm naturally, moving smoothly from your center. Bring your fist down to be emphatic, if you like, but don't bang.

Also, don't fidget—pulling your ear, twirling your hair, playing with jewelry, and an endless variety of attention-losers. Your voice, expression, gesture, and body are not separable.

7. *What to wear.* Choose an attractive and comfortable pantsuit or long dress with sleeves, and quiet jewelry. Be on guard with a short dress when crossing legs or bending down. Never chance a new outfit without a prior "dress rehearsal" before the meeting. Always take a jacket or sweater along just in case.

8. *If you use glasses.* Try extra-large type, or widely spaced capital letters. If they're no help, don't fret; you may choose contact lenses, half-glasses (to look over them at the audience), bifocals (these require eye coordination), or those chic glasses in large and interesting frames to complement the shape of your face. Of course, control the impulse to keep taking them off and putting them on.

Tensions, Away!

9. *A case of nerves.* Detect incipient nervousness in the act of slowing yourself down to a crawl; for the same reason, watch signs of accelerating the speed.

Don't panic if you lose your place; consult your script and *there it is;* never fear the moment of silence (the audience will catch up with you).

Breathe out frequently to counteract tension build-up (softly, during a pause).

For a dry mouth: drop your chin, opening your mouth slightly to release saliva; or hold a handkerchief to your mouth and run your tongue along the upper and lower teeth's gum line.

Final Touches

10. *Variety is the spice.* Help the audience to stay awake by changes in SPV (speed, pitch, volume). Eliminate another soporific, that dying inflection at the end of phrases.

11. *Go down, not up.* Learn to emphasize by favoring your lower, not throaty, range; as excitement mounts, your pitch may rise to shrillness. Pull your pitch down, but retain the volume for emphatic statements.

12. *Never hesitate to repeat* during a talk, an excellent form of emphasis. Let your sense of the dramatic prompt you when to re-iterate.

13. *Common static.* Refrain from clearing your throat repeatedly: people out front tend to echo the contagious sound. Get it over with: turn your face away from the audience and, covering mouth with your hand, cough.

The *er*'s and *um*'s: Cut down these common, irritating, habit-forming fillers between words. Pause instead, and proceed with what comes next (you probably ought to pause more, anyway).

14. *Sight plus sound.* Employ visual aids (charts, blackboards, slides) *if* they add to your talk. Make sure they stay out of sight until needed; rehearse the timing or your exhibit may become a handicap rather than an aid; steer clear of overwhelming the audience with too much detail.

15. *No cocktails, please.* Celebrate *after* the event. Skip a heavy repast beforehand (sidestep that luncheon invitation). Stay away from milk products (including ice cream). Singers always do.

16. *Watch the time.* Be guided by the minute hand of a *stopwatch* or a *timer* set to buzz just before your conclusion.

17. *An "up" ending.* Build to the finish. Don't drop off to tele-graph that the curtain's about to go down. Like a runner, summon your reserve energy to cross the finish line with a spurt (a sustained one).

It's Over

Your sensations are a jumble of relief, damp palms, exhilaration, and the sound of clapping. You come to in time to smile your thanks.

Friends gather around: "You sounded so natural—as if you were talking to each one of us individually." If they only knew how much preparation went into that talk!

It takes work to be "natural," to communicate with clear words linked together in a line of clear tone. Practice reduces anxiety to give you an *appearance* of ease, second best to *being* at ease. Naturalness also flows from letting down barriers by leveling with people, trusting them, and especially preparing for them.

16

TV, Radio, and the Lecture Circuit

We have covered the ground of live speech, from face to face with an audience of one, to person to person with gradually expanding numbers of listeners. Progressing (if that's the word) to TV and radio, with their awesome range of viewers and listeners, we discover, with no surprise, that the same basic speech concepts and skills apply. We need to accommodate what we already know particularly to the demands of television, now so enmeshed in the fabric of our lives.

Television

You've had the full treatment as viewer—years of looking and listening in on people who talk and move about on the small screen. The gap between you and them remains wide, though some of their faces have grown more familiar than your neighbor's. The immediacy of video contact, strong yet remote, poses a contradiction. What brings the four-inch people closer to us is what and how they communicate.

Note the stepped-up spurt of friendly, chatty, extended newscasts in local time slots. With "talking down from the heights" on the way out (apparently, no longer salable), more spontaneous and responsive talent has moved in, including women who increasingly make their presence felt. These current trends invite us to identify more directly with the performer on the small screen.

Once adjusted to the how-to's involved, you can make an almost painless transition to talking before an invisible audience—a logical extension of your speaking experience. Let us compare and clarify *the differences between platform and TV techniques:*

1. *Actually, appearing on TV is easier.* So much is done for you. The cameraman focuses in on *you* and the sound engineer tunes in *your voice*—both for maximum effectiveness. Another specialist helps with a flattering makeup to counteract the glare of bright lights that tend to wash out features. Ask a question and you'll be answered—the experts never object to making the routines clear.

2. *Everything on TV is more so.* Time is more rigid: on the platform, the timekeeper nudges you to conclude; on the air, you're simply cut off. More careful organization is called for. Your voice should be more conversational in tone, language more colloquial, expression more restrained, eye contact steadier, and your smile more of a twinkle.

Movements that would normally appear entirely natural are scaled down; larger gestures congenial to a platform would look ludicrous on the screen. You'll probably be confined to a chair with motion strictly limited (somewhat like sitting three abreast in a plane). The conventional "just relax" is not a cue to slump; sit more than ever erect, feeling the back of the chair with the middle of *your* back, and *appear* to relax.

3. *"The eyes have it."* As a long-time viewer you know how you feel uneasy with an unfocused gaze from the screen. So *look at the person* to whom you are speaking. If you want to pause and think, just change your sight lines slightly to the right or left, and then slowly return. *Shun any jerky action* of features, hand, or body. To *focus on the viewer,* direct your glance at the lens.

4. *Just about everything may show up in your speech.* When neophytes freeze on camera, rigidity may well come across in their voices. With hands tightly clasped, though out of sight, your tones will reflect the tenseness. Keep shoulders down, hands resting lightly on your lap or on the chair *(lightly* is the cue.). Once you attain an overall released feeling, the voice responds in kind. While the probing camera picks up negative signals, such as affectation, phoniness, bad manners, what a comfort to know the picture also reveals honesty, sincerity, and a feeling for people.

5. *Personal sound effects are too much!* Hands off the mike—some

people even tap it with a pencil. Don't beat a tattoo with your toes or drum on the table. Watch heavy breathing: a professional trick to imitate: to subdue the breath sounds effectively, *place the tip of your tongue behind your upper teeth as you inhale*—it's just that simple.

6. *You have to imagine the viewer.* The live contact you had on the platform, the give and take with an audience, is lost to TV. To compensate, always communicate on a one-to-one basis, holding the absent viewer constantly in mind, and pausing in natural speech rhythm as if to exchange thoughts.

7. *You want to look your informal best.* Some guidelines to dressing the part: underplay the clothes, be fussy about shape and fit; leave your busy prints and stark-white dresses at home (especially for color TV), along with flashy jewelry that catches TV lights or noisy, clunky bangles to compete with the sound equipment. Wear what's becoming, comfortable, and easy to *sit* in.

8. *The script takes special handling.* TV (and radio) permits little time for the gradual approach in speechmaking with its planned openers, buildups of proofs, and windups. Unlike the platform performance, *you can't:*

—count on five minutes to land a point; in video and audio delivery, it's more like a minute;

—start a train of thought that you can't finish in a hurry;

—repeat endlessly to clarify; repetition comes across in a tiresome rhythm;

—ease your way into a subject; instead, sharpen the angle and consider your every statement an answer to a question;

—risk losing the viewer/listener. Begin with an arresting phrase as you take off on a new thought.

To demonstrate: some sample openers for a "minute-to-minute" talk on today's trend of adhering to one's maiden name though married.

A rose by any other name. What's in a name? Everything! *It's you*—nothing in the law, marriage ceremony or license requires that a woman take her husband's name. Said Romeo, "Call me but love, and I'll be new baptized . . ."

Maiden name for a nonmaiden. Lucy Stone and Henry Blackwell married in 1855, together wrote the famous contract in which the bride retained her maiden name. Today more and more brides declare in their wedding announcements the intent to keep their own names after marriage.

"Husband and wife are one" and that one is the husband (or so it *was*). As alleged by traditionalists, are you "breaking up your home by keeping your own name?" How silly when you consider the high U.S. divorce rate! Sticking to husbands' names certainly hasn't preserved those families.

When you fill out a talk like this, continue with the same meaty yet spare approach.

Conscientious homework, as usual. For an *interview,* answer readily (you've probably been briefed on the questions). For a *round-table discussion,* have a few cards handy, especially for statistical material. For a *talk,* come furnished with script (to be used or not). Get off the page as much as possible, but don't be furtive by sneaking a look: take one.

Some pointers for mike expertise. The mike can be hung around your neck (the small necklace type), walked about followed by a long cord (the pencil type), dangled from a boom overhead, hidden in the artificial flowers, or just frankly deposited on the table. Watch these things:

—Most important: talk to people *as if the mike weren't there;* remember, it's just a convenience machine.

—Do not "project" your voice by pushing out sounds or words; talk as if to *one* person, *not* a mass.

—Control a breathy attack on consonants like /p/, /t/, /k/, /ch/, and sibiliant /s/'s and /sh/'s. Soft-pedal these sounds and at the same time lengthen key vowels—like this: "Be̲t̸t̸y Furne̸s̸s̸ (NBC News) g̲a̲ve c̸on̲s̲umers a s̸ha̲rp̸ les̸s̸on on pres̸c̸rip̸t̸ion dru̲g p̲ri̲c̸es̸."

—Stay with the volume level that you were told at the start was right for you; talk up and out and not into your lap.

Radio

Long before television, radio speakers and actors developed expert techniques for making the listener see the unseen scene. Versatile voices and ingenious sound effects told it all. Our radio sets have now shrunk to companionable size, waking us with news in the A.M. and lulling us to sleep with FM music at night.

Though drama has practically vanished (there's recently been a small revival), we can still hear good talk and other stimulating fare on the airwaves. Women have found on local stations a welcome and frequent outlet for airing small and large issues of concern to an attentive public. Tune in to listen for some attractive speech models.

Speaking on radio means sharpening all speech tools. The how-to's:

1. Modulate your tones as if talking to a friend across the table. Use hands and face and eyes; live expressions show up in voices.

2. Maintain an overall lively pace, and never push volume for emphasis; instead, emphasize by slowing the chosen word or phrase.

3. Imagine the listener in place and time: at home doing chores, at the office during coffee break, in a car during evening rush hour.

4. Read your script with our *off-the-page* techniques custom-made for radio. The listener can always tell when eyes remain riveted to the page. (Move papers separately and quietly, or slide each to the floor—an old radio gimmick.)

5. Present your ideas *as if they just occurred to you* (what theater people call "the illusion of the first time"). Caution: overlong silences sound deadly on radio.

6. Repeat points at intervals during a talk; someone may have just tuned in.

7. Pick up cues in an interview promptly, without hemming and hawing. Working with your cassette on the possible answers will have prepared you.

8. Remember, voice and words are all you have to go on! Radio is where practice pays off; invisible, you can concentrate on making full use of your gains in voice, enunciation, vocabulary, and poise.

After a TV or Radio Appearance—A Personal Checkup

—Were you on your best speech behavior, with all you've learned wrapped up and ready to use?

—Were you able to stand up to the goldfish-bowl exposure in the same way you managed to contain your fear on the platform?

—Was your concentration at the studio mainly on *what* you said and only subliminally on *how* you said it? Did you practice beforehand, confident that the effect would stay with you?

—Were you unperturbed by the bustle going on around you—the produc-

tion personnel, stagehands, time cues, signals, etc.? Since everybody was too busy to worry about you, did you *take care of yourself?*

Have Speech, Will Travel

At one time (eons before TV, it seems), *lecture circuits* crisscrossed the land. Today, right in the midst of the electronic giants, the live lecture business is booming again. The "hot properties"—famous columnists, muckrakers, former movie stars, Supreme Court justices, comedians with social fervor—a current mix of "names" (mostly men) commands large audiences and fees.

Lecture-goers find their ordinary entertainment on TV and look to the live speaker for something weightier, preferably with a controversial slant: the crises of energy, ecology, overpopulation, corruption in high places, consumer rebellion, and sexual revolution—subjects often expertly leavened with wit.

Time was when you were warmly welcomed as a *speakeress* (a believe-it-or-not item in the dictionary) if you could teach, in an entertaining manner, how to paint china, arrange flowers, raise African violets, or train myna birds. Nowadays women, talking with a more serious bent, are sought increasingly to highlight the program portions of assorted types of meetings.

In the present surge of cross-country lecturing, leading feminists, congresswomen, judges, poets, playwrights, critics, take to the road to meet the people voice to voice. Many of the top speakers consider their sizable fees subsidies for the freelance work they do. Others, without benefit of lecture agencies, find their own engagements in local areas, augmenting their incomes with smaller sums; and many dedicated women lecture for nothing or for a small honorarium.

As all of this speech activity gathers momentum, more women will grasp the opportunity to be heard, especially during political campaigns. Their speech consciousness raised, women who venture will discover that the way to upgrade personal communication is by *learning how* and *doing.*

Third Intermission for Vocal Refreshment

This reading-aloud excerpt is neither marked nor numbered, but you have the option of referring to p. 192 for those instructions. Or you may choose instead to deliver the monologue without further ado.

The classical Greek comedy *Lysistrata* was first produced in 411 B.C., at a moment when Athens' fortunes were at their lowest. In this celebrated ancient play with its many contemporary overtones, Aristophanes wrote his last, best plea for peace.

The plot: The women of Greece, led by the Athenian Lysistrata, unite in a sex strike, thus forcing their husbands to call off the war and fashion a just peace.

The scene: Having sent for the women from the other Greek city-states, Lysistrata addresses them. (Note: Several of her speeches have been blended into a condensed reading.)

Women of Sparta, Corinth, Thebes, and our Athenians, you ask me why I've sent for you—it's not an easy thing to tell. We must do something we have never done before, my friends. Something no woman, since the beginning of time, has dreamed of doing.

I ask, are you not sad and sorry that the fathers of your children are at the front—far away from you, in danger, without twenty-four hours' leave once in six months? Has any one of you seen her husband in the last half year?

If I bring your husbands back and end the war, will you be with me? If I show you the one way to end the war—if today, after this truce, they'll never march again—will you be with me?

My sisters, to compel our men to sign a pact of peace, we must make war—but not as men make war. Yet, be prepared for a great sacrifice. Oh, have no fears, it's not your lives you must give up. You'll only promise never to lie ... to lie with any man, until the war is ended. [*The passion in her tone startles them.*] Never to let a soldier home on leave, starved for your soft white arms and the great embrace of love, have joy of you until the war is over.

Hold yourself aloof! Abstain from love! Why, now you turn away! Where are you going? Back to wait your men's return, then let them go again to starve and kill and be killed, too.

Oh, women of Greece, stand together. We can forget our ancient wrongs, the lies they teach the children to make them hate their brothers. Stand by me!

When our men come home, what should we do? Can't you see it? First, we sit indoors and never run to meet them in the portico. They see the bright expectant flush upon our cheeks (the rouge pot serves for that) and when they come in, flinging their shield and spear upon the floor, we rise and our transparent gowns cling to our bodies. They go mad and fall upon us. Why, then, we turn away and say, "You must be tired," and talk about—the cobbler down the street, and say, "How nice to see you back," or "Did you have a good trip?" And then they *will* go mad. And if you tell them: "Never until the war is over"—*they'll make peace!*

Come, like the men, we'll swear a fearful oath: "Almighty goddess of the subtle tongue, mistress of argument, who gives victory in persuasion; Goddess of Love, whom we this once forswear; receive this sacrifice and be propitious to us women."

17

On the Campaign Trail

The British *stand* for office (good show!); we *run* (hurray!). In step with American tempo, women are making the *race* for city council all the way up to the governor's mansion. And beyond? Campaigning adds up to a speech marathon as candidates, organizers, and volunteers work and talk issues en route—hopefully, to victory.

In a time of shattering loss of faith in public morality and leadership, when most words and actions are suspect, women are raising hopeful issues relating to the *quality of life*. Straight, honest talk helps to heal the bitterness and to fill the political vacuum. There exists a reservoir of people's belief and hope waiting to be tapped. The country wants to come together—and must.

The new political woman is no longer willing just to organize box lunches and fried-chicken suppers, or content with the chores traditionally hers: stuffing envelopes, licking stamps, pounding pavements to get out the vote. She wants a piece of the action, to play the role of advocate as well as politician. Issue- and people-oriented, and articulate about the diminishing dollar, burdensome taxes, underpaid female labor force, and the threats to peace (national and world), her approach cuts through verbiage to the nub of questions.

Her affiliations are likely to be membership in the progressive wing of either major party, or a minority party, or independent of them all. While not necessarily an ideological feminist, she reflects the aura of newly found freedom, engendered by the women's movement, a term that begins to sound outmoded. Our new political woman's speech probably has a regional tinge, toned down; she works constantly to sustain and strengthen its clarity and content—and if she doesn't, *she should.*

The campaigners. The apparatus to elect anyone is a pyramid with the candidate at the apex and the volunteers at the broad base of the structure. In between are the political clubs, the citizens' and finance committees, the campaign staff of varied professional personnel, mainly women.

The candidate. She's not just any female party-liner, and will not inherit the office from her husband (an old, hand-me-down custom); our woman earns it on her own. This candidate prototype wins our endorsement because she:

—*knows how to win* (she has already learned how to lose);

—*appeals strongly* to minorities, women, reformers, consumers, the rank and file of labor, progressive business leaders;

—*has made her reputation* fighting for enlightened legislation in the state assembly and senate;

—*talks concretely* about the real-life problems of women and men (minus all bland rhetoric);

—*sparks* a creative campaign;

—*attracts a superior campaign staff* whose proficiency matches their devotion;

—*performs* as an effective speaker and phrasemaker (never coy or slippery);

—*makes public* her income-tax return;

—*inspires* women *as a role model* to vote for her across party lines;

—*exhibits grace* under pressure.

But is she qualified? This all too familiar question, directed at the woman who aspires to office, is a put-down that masks the opposition to her candidacy. A woman who has reached the point of potential nomination has already amply demonstrated her eligibility as a lawyer, an executive, and/or a specialist in community problems, plus her track record in political affairs. To put it differently, it took some going to get there in the first place!

The main hurdle she faces is to gain the nomination; party leaders dictate that decision and it often takes great pressure from the constituency to ensure her a place on the ballot. Women have a good record of winning—when they run.

Another bind: A candidate isn't considered seriously until she can raise large sums of campaign money, and she can't raise money until she's considered seriously! And so it goes, nip and tuck to the finish line.

The volunteer. "It's dirty, back-room business, I don't want to soil my hands, it doesn't work, nobody's going to listen, and what can one person do anyway?": the echoing excuses for staying out of the political process (and to keep from speaking up?). Some of these same skeptics eventually learn to enjoy six hours of envelope-stuffing in the company of a group of enthusiastic volunteers.

Volunteers are the life's blood of any campaign; they believe in the democratic political system and make it work for the best candidate—*theirs.* The woman running for office, of course, can never get around to all of the electorate, but her representatives (the staff and volunteers) almost do. Training sessions in campaign management (largely speech skills) have begun to change the image of the volunteer from a reliable "gofer" to an effective campaigner.

From top to bottom. The campaign network picks up speed as the election nears, reaching fever heat when that day dawns—at last, the moment-to-moment mobilization to round up the lagging vote. Nothing is more hectic!

If the candidate wins, the workers share a boost to their self-esteem; if she makes a good showing and loses, they weep, but there's always next time. And if she winds up at the tail end of the scoreboard, almost everyone can agree that, in promoting the candidate and the issues, and in making the campaign audible and visible, they have helped to change the political climate (no small feat).

Winning voices. An election campaign is a microcosm of intensified speaking situations. Assuredly, the higher the reach of speech expertise, the more dynamism a campaign conveys.

The women involved, from candidate to volunteer, seek improved ways and means to communicate—with the electorate, with the media, with each other. To promote cause and candidate, the existing speaker's bureau calls upon a proven list of speechmakers, already experienced, and always in short supply. And too often, unfortunately, the rest of the campaigners lag behind, making do with lackluster skills—a situation begging for correction.

The daily grind of talk—planning, arguing, crusading—beats up voices. With the pressure on vocal cords, hoarseness sets in, and the result?—a disabled campaigner.

We certainly don't wish to restrict the anger against injustice or honest passion in a cause that can move and stir the listener. But uncontrolled emotion minus proper bodily support constricts the throat.

Preventive pointers for zealous campaigners. At meetings, stop clearing your throat, and catch that scratchiness before it worsens. While waiting your turn to speak, that classic aid, yawning, will release laryngeal tensions—not, however, in full view of listeners! Try a yawn or two behind a printed leaflet, or beforehand, when taking a walk around the block. On the platform, or not, breathe in and out rhythmically. Spare your throat as you speak. Take an easy breath between phrases, riding your words on the breath.

On-the-bandwagon skills covering the whole range of skills throughout these pages:

Conversation: The heart of all good speaking: informed citizens airing key issues throughout the constituency, and triggering, particularly among women, a collective spirit for victory.

Interviews: Upgraded, grass-roots canvassing, door to door and via telephone; enlisting backers—women/men leaders in education, the arts, trade unions.

Group discussions: Thrashing out policy and programs (not rap sessions); intensive political round tables.

Panels: Rousing forums for campaign meetings; taking advantage of "equal time," feisty TV and radio debates with opposition candidates.

The solo public speech: Heightened, responsible conversation for all "soloists." The candidate's chief concern: the ability to present herself and the campaign program cogently, strongly, even eloquently; as she stumps county, state, or cross-country, the rules recommended for preparation and delivery, including those for TV and radio, operate in high gear. Electioneering forthrightly, our standard bearer sets the tone and style for co-workers and supporters who speak in her behalf.

In the midst of all this, the candidate has learned that:

—speaking is an art of persuasion, and sincerity, the touchstone;

—people have gut reactions to voices: brash and abrasive tones turn them off;

—the venting of defensive emotions may embarrass the listener.

Her *manner* projects neither too much humility nor overconfidence—never apologetic, hesitant, or overcompensating. Her *pace* avoids the laborious, thinking-everything-out approach as well as rapid-fire breathlessness. Her *words* never talk down to people; she figuratively gets off the platform to level with them. Her *language*, above everything, has substance—concise, colloquial (not cozy). Her *voice*, modulated yet clearly audible, engages the listener.

For every woman who achieves such levels of excellence, there are numerous others who never had or sought the opportunities. Campaigning unleashes the energies and aspirations of women as communicating citizens. By spreading the message of progressive political change, they reach a high point of self-expression.

In urgent demand: More and more articulate voices—practiced, appealing—developed, wherever possible, in speech workshops set up well in advance of a campaign. From such groups we can anticipate the fluent and clear-voiced advocates and candidates for the coming political melees.

The Accelerating Scene

The kaleidoscopic seventies are spinning off one "would-you-believe" development after another. The events have crowded out from the women's page and spilled over into all sections of the daily paper: WOMAN JOCKEY WINS AT AQUEDUCT, WOMEN IN MEDICINE—A DRAMATIC RISE, ELEVEN WOMEN ORDAINED AS PRIESTS, WOMAN'S NOMINATION AS GOVERNOR ENSURES ELECTION (so what else is *old?*). While the picture still shows spots more gray than rosy, the gains are here to stay, never to be relinquished, with plenty more on the way. And there remain few areas where haphazard speaking is not a drawback—even the jockeys have to talk to the horses!

One Last Word

A youthful out-of-towner, lost in the New York subway on her way to a concert, emerged in desperation to find herself on the Lower East Side. "Excuse me," she asked the first person she met. "How do I get to Carnegie Hall?"

The old man regarded her for a moment. "Practice," he answered, "practice!"

Selected Bibliography

American English

Alexander, Henry. *The Story of Our Language.* New York: Anchor (Double-day), 1969.

Barnett, Lincoln. *The Treasure of Our Tongue.* New York: Mentor (NAL), 1967.

Mencken, H. L. *The American Language: An Inquiry into the Development of English in the United States.* 3rd edition. New York: Knopf, 1926.

Body Language

Eisenberg, Abner, and Smith, Ralph R., Jr. *Nonverbal Communication.* New York: Bobbs-Merrill, 1971.

Conversation

Walters, Barbara. *How to Talk to Practically Anybody about Practically Anything.* New York: Dell, 1971.

Discussion

Brilhart, John K. *Effective Group Discussion* (Speech Communication Series). Dubuque, Iowa: Wm. C. Brown, 1967.

Lee, Irving J. *How to Talk with People.* New York: Harper & Row, 1952.

Family Talk

Ginott, Haim G. *Between Parent and Child.* New York: Macmillan, 1965.

Gordon, Thomas. *P.E.T.: Parent Effectiveness Training*. New York: Wyden, 1974.

Sarson, Evelyn, general ed. *Action for Children's Television*. The first national symposium on the effect of television programming and advertising on children. New York: Discuss (Avon), 1971.

Tooze, Ruth. *Storytelling*. New York: Prentice-Hall, 1960.

Van Riper, Charles. *Your Child's Speech Problems*. New York: Harper, 1961.

Parliamentary Procedure

Keesey, Ray E. *Modern Parliamentary Procedure*. Boston: Houghton, Mifflin, 1974. (Especially chapters 3, 4, and 7.)

Sturgis, Alice. *Standard Code of Parliamentary Procedure*. New York: McGraw-Hill, 1966.

Reading-aloud Materials

Chester, Laura, and Barba, Sharon, eds. *Rising Tides, 20th Century American Women Poets*. New York: Washington Square Press (Pocket), 1973.

Coger, Leslie Irene, and White, Melvin R., ed. *Readers Theatre Handbook, A Dramatic Approach to Literature*. Rev. ed. Lakeville, Ill.: Scott, Foresman, 1973.

Mattingly, Althea S., and Grimes, Wilma H. *Interpretation: Writer—Reader —Audience*. Belmont, Calif.: Wadsworth, 1970.

Murray, Michele, ed. *A House of Good Proportion: Images of Women in Literature*. New York: Simon & Schuster, 1973.

Non-stereotyped girl/boy books

Some few suggestions for *little* children:

Schick, Eleanor. *City in the Winter*. New York, Macmillan, 1970.

Zolotow, Charlotte. *William's Doll*. New York, Harper and Row, 1972.

For *middle-aged* children:

A Bibliography/Catalogue of Non-Sexist Children's Literature. Whitestone, N.Y., Feminist Book Mart, 1974.

Cleaver, Vera and Bill. *Grover*. Philadelphia, Lippincott, 1970.

Sachs, Marilyn. *The Truth About Mary Rose*. New York, Doubleday, 1973.

In addition to the publishers already listed, these firms have been turning out excellent children's books: Atheneum, T.Y. Crowell, Lollypop Power (Chapel Hill, N.C.), Scholastic Book Services, and The Viking Press. Catalogues on request from the publishers.

For Listening

The spoken word recording companies are now producing cassette tapes as well as disks. A wide variety of stories, poetry, and plays for children and adults are spoken and performed by skilled readers and actors. Some fine labels include: Caedmon Records, Folkways, Scholastic Tapes and Spoken Arts. Tapes and disks are available at many public libraries.

Speech

Brigance, William Norwood. *Speech Communication*, 3d ed. Revised by J. Jeffery Auer. New York: Appleton-Century-Crofts, 1967.

Eisenson, Jon. *The Improvement of Voice and Diction*. London: Collier-Macmillan, 1965.

Fairbanks, Grant. *Voice and Articulation Drillbook*. New York: Harper & Row, 1960.

Prochnow, Herbert V., and Prochnow, Herbert V., Jr. *A Treasury of Humorous Quotations for Speakers, Writers and Home Reference*. New York: Harper & Row, 1969.

Vital Speeches of the Day. Southold, L.I., N.Y.: City News, Publishing Company. A bimonthly periodical.

Vocabulary

Lewis, Norman. *New Guide to Word Power*. New York: Pyramid, 1969.

Newman, Edwin. *Strictly Speaking*. New York: Bobbs-Merrill, 1974.

Nurnberg, Maxwell, and Rosenblum, Morris. *All About Words: An Approach to Vocabulary Building*. Englewood Cliffs, N.J.: Prentice-Hall, 1966.

Voice Therapy

Brodnitz, Friedrich S. *Keep Your Voice Healthy*. New York: Harper & Row, 1953.

Greene, Margaret C. L. *The Voice and Its Disorders*. New York: Pitman, 1972.

Van Riper, Charles, and Irwin, John V. *Voice and Articulation.* Englewood
    Cliffs, N.J.: Prentice-Hall, 1958.

Women: Background and Life-styles

Beauvoir, Simone de. *The Second Sex.* New York: Knopf, 1953.

Flexner, Eleanor. *Century of Struggle: The Women's Rights Movement in the
    United States.* New York: Atheneum, 1973.

Gorney, Sondra, and Cox, Claire. *After Forty: How Women Can Achieve
    Fulfillment.* New York: Dial, 1973.

Klagsbrun, Francine, ed. *The Ms. Reader.* New York: Warner Paperback,
    1973.

Mead, Margaret, and Kaplan, Frances Blagley, eds. *American Women: The
    Report of the President's Commission on the Status of Women and
    Other Publications of the Commission.* With an Introduction and
    Epilogue by Margaret Mead. New York: Scribners, 1965.

Schaefer, Leah Cahan. *Women and Sex.* New York: Pantheon, 1973. (Includes
    a comprehensive bibliography.)

Tolchin, Martin and Susan. *Clout: Women Power and Politics.* New York:
    Coward, McCann & Geoghegan, 1974.

Catalyst: Career Opportunity Series, prepared by the New York chapter of
    the Women's National Book Association, 6 East 82nd Street, New
    York, N.Y. 10028. Pamphlet titles include: Banking, Communica-
    tions, Data Processing, Engineering, Environmental Affairs, Law,
    Publishing, Your Job Campaign, among many others. From 1973,
    an ongoing excellent series.

Index

Index

Dorothy Uris

at the age of eleven joined a debating team in her native Brooklyn. ("That's how come I speak so well.") After studying at Cornell, she became a professional actress in theater and films, some thirty of them, as Dorothy Tree ("I left *her* in Hollywood"). Then she came back to New York and to Teacher's College at Columbia University, which led to the second career, as a teacher of voice and speech, a coach, and a writer. A Martha Baird Rockefeller grant sent her on wide-ranging research into linguistics and English diction. Her book *To Sing in English*, a singers' and actors' standard, was the result.

Besides teaching at the Mannes College of Music and the Manhattan School of Music, Ms. Uris functions actively as a therapist, speech correctionist, and specialist in public speaking and the skills of reading aloud. Her son Joe is a (well-spoken) psychiatric social worker.